Using Ubuntu Linux

Other Titles of Interest from Bernard Babani (publishing) Ltd

BP579 Upgrading To and Troubleshooting Windows Vista

BP580 Windows Vista for Beginners

BP581 Windows Vista Explained

BP583 Microsoft Office 2007 Explained

BP614 Computing with Vista for the Older Generation

Other Titles by the same author

BP565	Using Microsoft Windows XP Media Center 2005
BP567	How To Set Up Your Home or Small Business Network
BP571	Getting More From Your Microsoft Xbox 360
BP578	Microsoft Windows Vista – An Ultimate Guide

Using Ubuntu Linux

by

Jon Rolfe

&

Andrew Edney

Bernard Babani (publishing) Ltd

The Grampians

Shepherds Bush Road

London W6 7NF

England

www.babanibooks.com

Please Note

Although every care has been taken with the production of this book to ensure that any projects, designs, modifications and/or programs, etc. contained herewith, operate in a correct and safe manner and also that any components specified are normally available in Great Britain, the Publishers and Author(s) do not accept responsibility in any way for the failure (including fault in design) of any project, design, modification or program to work correctly or to cause damage to any equipment that it may be connected to or used in conjunction with, or in respect of any other damage or injury that may be so caused, nor do the Publishers accept responsibility in any way for the failure to obtain specified components.

Notice is also given that if equipment that is still under warranty is modified in any way or used or connected with home-built equipment then that warranty may be void.

ISBN 978 0 85934 586 6

© 2007 BERNARD BABANI (publishing) LTD

First Published – September 2007

British Library Cataloguing in Publication Data

A catalogue record for this book is available from the British Library

Cover design by Gregor Arthur

Printed and bound in Great Britain by J. H. Haynes & Co. Ltd., Sparkford

About this Book

Welcome to Using Ubuntu Linux, and thank you for buying this book. We hope it will be an invaluable source of information and guidance in order for you to setup, configure and discover the secure, feature rich, and easy to use operating system that is Ubuntu Desktop.

Most books on GNU/Linux based operating systems have been aimed at technical computer users, or users who have wanted to increase their technical knowledge. While writing this book, we have aimed to provide a resource for the everyday, non-technical user, who just wants to use their computer as the tool it was designed for.

This book will try to avoid long lists of manual commands that must be typed at a flashing prompt, unless they are absolutely necessary. Thankfully when the subject has been voted as the most user friendly Linux based operating system (voted Most User-Friendly Linux Distribution, and Best Linux/Open Source Distribution, for the second year running, at the 2006 UK Linux and Open Source Awards), long confusing commands are very rare and can easily be avoided.

We hope you enjoy the journey.

Conventions

Throughout this book, you will see a number of information boxes, bounded with either a double line like this...

DESIGNATING A WARNING

...or indeed, a single line, like this...

DESIGNATING A NOTE, POINT OF INTEREST OR USEFUL TIP

Procedures and walkthroughs may be shown as numerical lists, like this:

1. Step 1
2. Step 2

All diagrams and Figures have a two-digit reference number containing the Chapter number, followed by the Figure number within that Chapter. For example, Figure 1-1 represents the first Figure in Chapter 1.

About the Authors

Jon Rolfe has been an IT professional for over 12 years, working for some of the largest global IT services companies such as Fujitsu and EDS. During his career he has specialised in Microsoft based solutions and provided design, architecture and development experience for large enterprise solutions for numerous blue-chip organisations and government departments. Jon has an extensive knowledge of IT systems, with experience spanning from the early Sinclair ZX81, through PCs, Macs, Windows and Linux.

Jon lives in Hampshire and has an active interest in IT, consumer electronics, digital photography and motor sport. When he gets the chance he also enjoys Mountain Biking and Skiing.

He can be contacted through the Using Ubuntu website (http://UsingUbuntu.com) or emailed at Jon@UsingUbuntu.com.

Andrew Edney has been an IT consultant for over 12 years and over the course of his career has worked for a range of high-tech companies, such as Microsoft, Hewlett Packard and Fujitsu Services. He has a wide range of experience in virtually all aspects of Microsoft's computing solutions, having designed and architected large enterprise solutions for government and private sector customers. Over the years, Andrew had made a number of guest appearances at major industry events, presenting on a wide range of Information Systems subjects, such as an appearance at the annual

Microsoft Exchange Conference in Nice where he addressed the Microsoft technical community on Mobility Computing. Andrew is currently involved in numerous Microsoft beta programmes, including next generation Windows operating systems and next generation Microsoft Office products, and actively participates in all Windows Media Center beta programmes. On top of all of this, Andrew runs his own IT consulting company, Firebird Consulting and has currently authored eight books and is busy working on more.

Andrew lives in Wiltshire with his partner, Katy, and their two cats and can be reached at andrew@firebirdconsulting.co.uk.

Acknowledgements

We would like to offer my thanks to our family and friends for their support and assistance during the long months of writing this book. In addition, we would also like to offer our thanks to all the staff at Babani for publishing our book.

To my father for his 70th birthday

- Jon

Trademarks

Ubuntu and **Canonical** are registered trademarks of Canonical Ltd.

All other brand names and product names used in this book are recognised as trademarks, or registered trademarks of their respective companies.

Contents

PART 4 Troubleshooting

PART 1
An Introduction to Ubuntu Linux

1

Introduction

To provide a background on the Ubuntu operating system, it is necessary to give a brief history lesson on the UNIX and GNU/Linux operating systems. This chapter hopes to provide you with a little background knowledge to explain how Ubuntu has evolved from its UNIX ancestors and GNU/Linux cousins. It will also go on to explain the philosophy behind Ubuntu, and explain the many derivatives of the most user-friendly GNU/Linux operating system that is available today.

A Brief History

UNIX

The UNIX operating system was originally born in the late 1960s from research carried out by AT&T Bell Telephone Laboratories on the Multics project. This project, meaning Multiplexed Information and Computing Service was a joint collaboration of Bell Labs, General Electric and the

Massachusetts Institute of Technology. The aim of the project was to provide a reliable "time-sharing" operating system for a large computer which could be used by numerous users.

Early attempts proved complex and unsuccessful and a small team from the original project broke away and rewrote the operating system for a smaller system. The project was renamed UNICS for Uniplexed Information and Computing Service, somewhere along the way this name was changed to UNIX. By the early 1970s the UNIX operating system had started to be used within AT&T, and was made available to Universities, the United States Government and some commercial organisations under a licence that included the source code of the operating system.

By the late 1970s, the operating system had begun to be used extensively as an academic tool, and as the graduate students left to join commercial organisations they wished to continue using the UNIX OS. This resulted in companies being setup (such as Sun Microsystems and Santa Cruz Operation or SCO) and developing their own versions under licence from AT&T.

Today, many large computer systems around the world run the mature, reliable and secure operating system from companies such as Sun Microsystems, HP and IBM.

The GNU Project and Linux

In 1983, Richard Stallman launched the GNU Project (http://www.gnu.org) to develop a UNIX like operating system which was free to use. Stallman was a developer at the

Artificial Intelligence Lab at MIT, and was the inventor of the EMACS editor. The project was named GNU (pronounced guh-noo) to be a recursive acronym for "GNU's Not UNIX".

He had strongly held beliefs that all software should be free, which had been formed from his years at MIT in the 1970s when the limited software in the academic environment was developed and distributed freely. By the 1980s and the commercialisation of the UNIX operating system, GNU was born to provide an operating system and suite of applications that could again be freely distributed. In 1985 the Free Software Foundation (http://www.fsf.org) was formed primarily to raise money to aid the development of the GNU project.

In 1991, development of the GNU system was still in progress and it was not yet available. However, Linus Torvalds had developed a UNIX compatible kernel (the central or core part of an operating system) and named it Linux. This was combined with the GNU system in 1992 to create the GNU/Linux system which is the ancestor of the many "Linux" (more correctly call GNU/Linux) based operating systems available today.

Ubuntu

The Ubuntu operating system is named after an African word (pronounced oo-BOON-too) which loosely means "humanity to others" or "I am what I am because of who we all are". The Ubuntu operating system aims to bring this ideal to the software world. Or, more simply, this is summed up as "Linux for Human Beings".

The operating system was first started in April 2004 by Mark Shuttleworth, a South African Internet entrepreneur, who put together a small team of open source developers with the aim of releasing a user-friendly and free operating system for all. Quoting the Ubuntu Community (http://www.ubuntu.com/community/ubuntustory/philosophy), the operating system is based on the following philosophy or belief:

- *Every computer user should have the freedom to download, run, copy, distribute, study, share, change and improve their software for any purpose, without paying licensing fees.*

- *Every computer user should be able to use their software in the language of their choice.*

- *Every computer user should be given every opportunity to use software, even if they work under a disability.*

The first release was launched in October 2004 and was named version 4.10. It was a development of an existing GNU/Linux distribution called Debian (http://www.debian.org) but had the aim of providing a more user-friendly system than other GNU/Linux based systems at the time. Debian was started by

Ian Murdock in 1993 and was the name of one of many GNU/Linux versions, its aim was to provide a repository of free GNU software that was collected, packaged and supported.

Ubuntu has a commitment of regular six monthly releases and these are named slightly differently to the other software releases. All releases are named from the year and month of release, so version 4.10 was released in the tenth month of 2004. At the time of writing the current release is version 7.04, released in April 2007.

Along with the unique version numbering, the Ubuntu operating system has code names for each operating system release. As the initial v4.10 release was an early development it was nicknamed "Warty Warthog". The current development release is codenamed "Gutsy Gibbon" and is due for release in October 2007, to be officially known as Ubuntu 7.10.

Ubuntu Features

Many people might question why yet another GNU/Linux release was needed, as there are many already available from commercial organisations such as Red Hat and Novell, as well as free versions such as Slackware. Along with the belief of free software for all, including developing countries, the Ubuntu system had the aim of a fully featured and user friendly operating system, as many of the existing free or commercial versions were very powerful but aimed at technical users.

Ubuntu was therefore designed to be as user friendly as any commercial operating system such as Microsoft Windows or Mac OS X. It was also designed to be usable and secure straight after installation. So the system is pre-installed with the most common applications users will need, such as:

- A suite of applications for word processing, spreadsheets, databases and presentations
- Internet tools for web browsing, email and instant messaging
- Graphics tools for editing and managing pictures
- Multimedia tools for playing videos and music.

Since security has become of great importance in recent years, the Ubuntu system was also designed to be as secure as possible without lengthy configuration. It therefore has the aim to provide only the tools and services required for a workstation and aims to disable by default, facilities that are usually not required. This doesn't mean it lacks functionality; simply the functionality must be enabled when required so that the system is kept as secure as possible. To further enhance security, the system supports automatic detection of security updates and will prompt the user when they are available. Of course, this security feature is also on by default so that systems are kept secure without the user needing to configure it.

After three years of development, Ubuntu is rapidly becoming the defacto free GNU/Linux distribution. Some of the numerous awards and accolades that it has received have been:

- Wins a "100 Best Products of 2007" Award from PC World magazine in May 2007

- Chosen as an option to be pre-installed on new Dell PCs and Laptops in May 2007

- Receives "Editors Choice Award" from PC Welt magazine in March 2007

- Wins "Most User Friendly Linux Distribution Award" at the Linux New Media Awards in November 2006

- Chosen as "Best Linux/Open Source Distribution", at the UK Linux and Open Source Awards in October 2006, for the second year in succession.

Ubuntu Versions

Today, Ubuntu is available in several flavours, each tuned for a particular use.

Ubuntu Desktop

Ubuntu Desktop (http://www.ubuntu.com) is the primary version of the operating system, however, this too is available in different types. This version is based on a desktop environment called "Gnome" and is the version this book is based upon. However, many of the steps and tips are equally relevant for the other versions also based on the Gnome desktop environment.

Kubuntu

However, another version called Kubuntu (http://www.kubuntu.org) is also released at the same time as the main Ubuntu releases. This is based on a different desktop environment call KDE or K Desktop Environment, and so supports a different variety of applications that have been developed for this desktop environment.

Edubuntu

Edubuntu (http://www.edubuntu.org) is based on Ubuntu, but comes with a suite of applications designed for children and education, and is summed up with the phrase "Linux for Young Human Beings"!

Xubuntu

Like Kubuntu, Xubuntu (http://www.xubuntu.org) is based on the Ubuntu system but uses the Xfce Desktop Environment. This gives the system a slightly different look and feel and a different suite of applications. The main advantage of Xubuntu is the Xfce desktop environment requires less system resources than the Gnome environment used for Ubuntu. It is therefore ideal for older, less powerful hardware.

Ubuntu Studio

A relatively new release, Ubuntu Studio (http://ubuntustudio.com) is an optimised Ubuntu Desktop release for media creation. The system has had additional development to avoid latency for time critical applications used for music or video editing. It also comes pre-installed with a suite of applications dedicated to graphics, video and music editing.

Ubuntu Server

Finally, we come to Ubuntu Server (http://www.ubuntu.com). As the name suggests, this release is optimised for performing server tasks such as for web, email or database server tasks. To save memory and resources, this version does not come with a desktop environment and so must be installed, configured and administered from a command line.

Ubuntu Support

Each Ubuntu release is developed by the Ubuntu community, a team of developers across the world who collaborate to develop and update the Ubuntu operating system. Released every six months, each version has a commitment to be supported for at least 18 months by the Ubuntu community. However, there are occasionally releases known as "Long Term Support" or LTS releases such as Ubuntu 6.06. These versions are released to ensure that frequent re-installation of operating system upgrades is not required. The long term support releases will be supported for a minimum of three years for the desktop and five years for servers.

Apart from development and fixes, the Ubuntu community also develops the on-line help, and provides support forums for free help and advice. The community is also backed by the commercial company Canonical Ltd, started by Mark Shuttleworth. The company provides commercial support, training and certification on the free operating system for users and commercial companies who require a service beyond that which can be provided by the community.

Summary

In this chapter we have covered a brief history to help provide an understanding of where Ubuntu has come from, and its belief in providing a user-friendly, feature rich operating system that is based on the early ideals of the GNU project of being freely available for all. In the following chapters we get to grips with installing the operating system and trying it out for real.

PART 2
Setup

2

Setup

In this chapter, we take our first steps into the free software world and we test Ubuntu on our computer, before committing to installing it.

> Don't worry, the installation is an easy process and shouldn't take more than 30 minutes.

Installing Ubuntu

Once you're ready to try Ubuntu, the first task is to obtain the CD. This is freely available to download from the Ubuntu website (http://www.ubuntu.com/getubuntu/download). The download file is an ISO CD image (an industry standard file format for CDs) that can be written to a blank CD by most CD writing software. If you don't have access to a broadband Internet connection necessary to download the CD image, it is also possible to buy the Ubuntu installation CD for a small fee from various companies that can be found on the Internet (http://www.ubuntu.com/getubuntu/purchase).

> Before installation, it is important to ensure that you back up all your work files (either to CD, USB memory stick or USB hard disc), as the installation process will erase your hard disc.

Testing Your System Hardware

The Ubuntu CD is called a "live" CD as it is possible to boot (or start-up) your computer into Ubuntu Desktop from the CD before installation onto your computers hard disc. This allows you to test the computers hardware for compatibility, or to just give Ubuntu a test drive before overwriting your existing operating system.

To start your computer from the live CD, place the CD into your CD-Rom drive and restart your computer. When the system starts up, the system should start from the CD and load Ubuntu. If this does not happen, it may be necessary to select the computers "boot menu" just after the computer is switched on. This is often displayed by a message such as "Press F12 for start menu" which will result in a boot menu being displayed as shown in Figure 2-1.

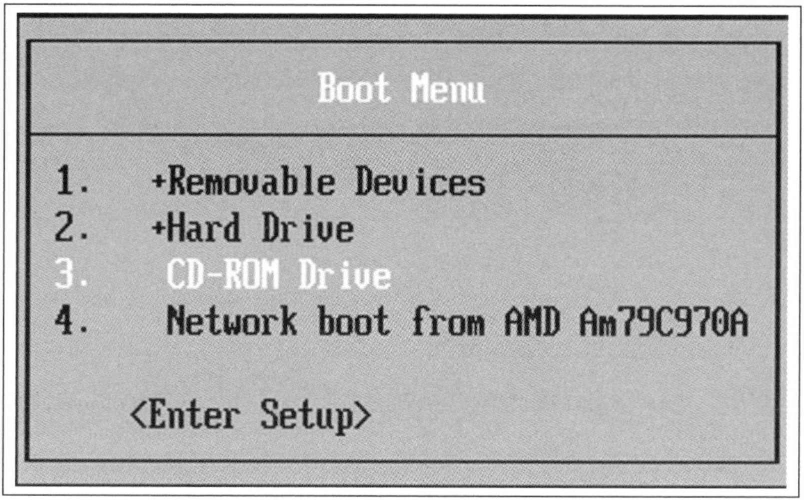

```
┌─────────────────────────────────────────────┐
│  ┌───────────────────────────────────────┐  │
│  │            Boot Menu                   │  │
│  ├───────────────────────────────────────┤  │
│  │  1.   +Removable Devices               │  │
│  │  2.   +Hard Drive                      │  │
│  │  3.    CD-ROM Drive                    │  │
│  │  4.    Network boot from AMD Am79C970A │  │
│  │                                        │  │
│  │       <Enter Setup>                    │  │
│  └───────────────────────────────────────┘  │
└─────────────────────────────────────────────┘
```

Figure 2-1 BIOS Boot Menu

Select the CD by pressing the relevant number and the system will start loading Ubuntu desktop. During the loading, a menu will be displayed providing various options, as can be seen in Figure 2-2.

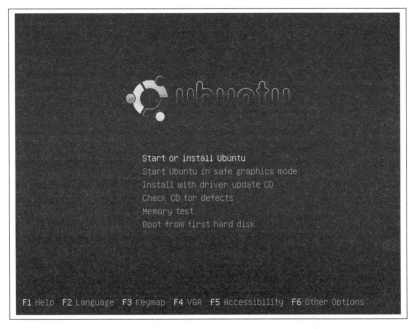

Figure 2-2 Live CD Startup Menu

Before installing from the CD, it is recommended to select the "Check CD for defects" option to ensure that the image file has been correctly written to the CD. Select this option by using the up and down arrows and pressing return. If a defect is detected, remove the CD and reboot into your existing Operating System and write the image file to another CD and try again. Once the CD image has been verified, select the "Start or install Ubuntu" option to load the Ubuntu Desktop operating system.

While the system is loading, an Ubuntu "splash" screen will be displayed along with a progress bar. After a little while, the Ubuntu desktop will be displayed as shown in Figure 2-3.

Figure 2-3 Ubuntu Live CD Desktop

Take a while to investigate the Ubuntu Desktop, and to make sure that your system is working correctly. The system will feel a little slow while running from the live CD, as a CD drive is much slower than a hard disc.

Open the examples folder on the desktop and try opening some of the sample files such as the "Experience

Ubuntu.ogg" file to ensure that the Ubuntu Operating System can play videos and movies on your system.

Installation

Once you're happy that your system's keyboard, mouse, display and sound are all working correctly, and that you have backed up all your existing files, it is time to start installing your new system. To start the installation, double-click the "Install" icon on the desktop.

The Installation Welcome screen will now be displayed, as shown in Figure 2-4. Select your language and press the forward button to continue the installation process.

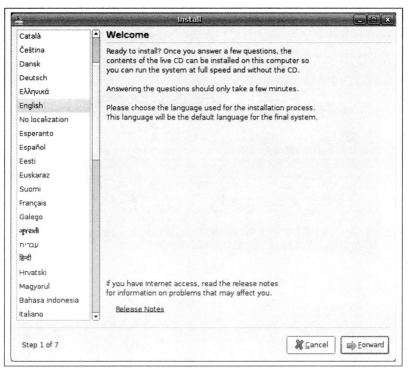

Figure 2-4 Welcome Screen

You will now be prompted to select your location, as shown in Figure 2-5. Click on the world map to zoom in and then select your location on the map. When you are happy that you have selected the correct location press the "Forward" button.

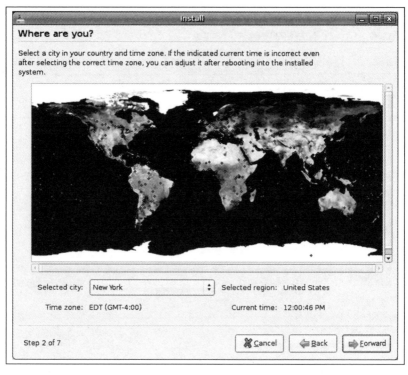

Figure 2-5 Choosing where you are in the world

Next, select your keyboard layout from the options list as shown in Figure 2-6.

> Type a few words of text to ensure that your keyboard works correctly, making sure that the special characters or symbols for your language or region work correctly.

When you are happy that everything works as you would expect it to press the "Forward" button again to continue.

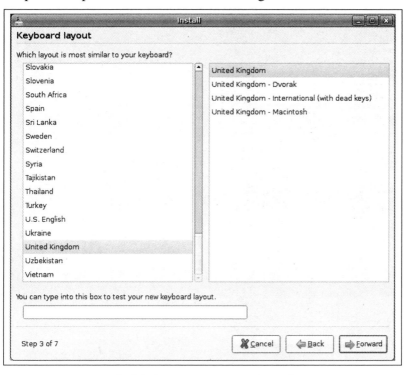

Figure 2-6 Selecting your Keyboard Layout

You will then be prompted to select the partitioning scheme for your hard disc, as shown in Figure 2-7.

It is recommended to select the "guided" option which will configure the recommended partitioning layout for your system.

If you have more than one hard disc installed in your computer, select the relevant disc under the "guided" option and press "Forward" to continue.

Figure 2-7 Select your partitioning scheme

It is also possible to install Ubuntu alongside your existing Operating System, rather than replacing it. Because Ubuntu uses a different format for the hard disc than Windows, to do this you must make spare space on your hard disc.

If anything goes wrong during this operation, you may lose your existing operating system! Make sure you have saved all your important files first.

To resize your existing partition, select the "Manual" option. You can then choose to resize your existing hard disc "partition" by first selecting the partition and then clicking "Edit Partition". Enter a new size for the partition in megabytes and press OK.

Figure 2-8 Partition Edit

Next, you'll need to create a swap partition. Highlight the newly created free space, click "New Partition", enter the size to create as 2,000MB, and choose "Swap". Click the available free space again, and then click "New Partition", and choose "/" or root, and select the format as "ext3". Leave the other settings alone and press "Next".

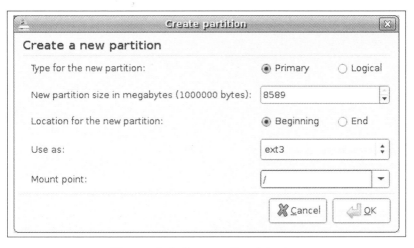

Figure 2-9 Custom Partitioning

A new feature with Ubuntu 7.04 is the ability for the installer to migrate your user settings if you are installing on a system that is already installed with Windows, as shown in Figure 2-10. As you can see from Figure 2-10 there were no users or operating systems suitable for importing from, but if there were they would be displayed here.

Figure 2-10 Migrate Documents and Settings

If you do not want to migrate the user settings, simply press forward. Otherwise select a user listed in the Migrate Documents and Settings dialog and a username and password for the new Ubuntu account to use with these settings before pressing "Forward".

Next, enter your name, password and the name you wish to give to your computer, as shown in Figure 2-11, before pressing the "Forward" button.

> Make sure you choose a complex password (such as a mixture of letters and characters) to ensure your computer is kept secure.

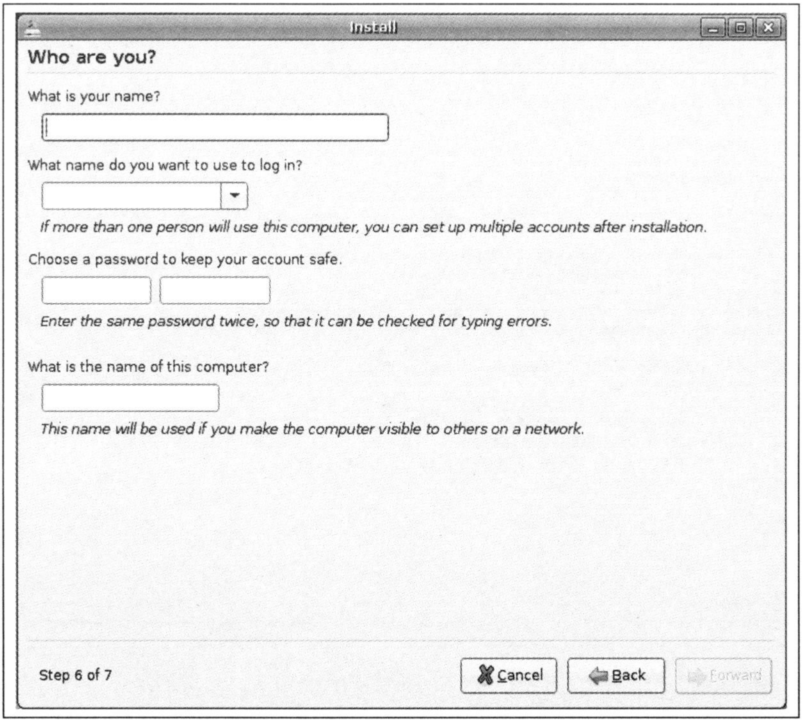

Figure 2-11 Entering your user details

Finally, a summary screen will be displayed allowing you to change the options you have selected, as shown in Figure 2-12. If you are happy with your choices and you have backed up your existing files, press the "Install" button to commence the installation.

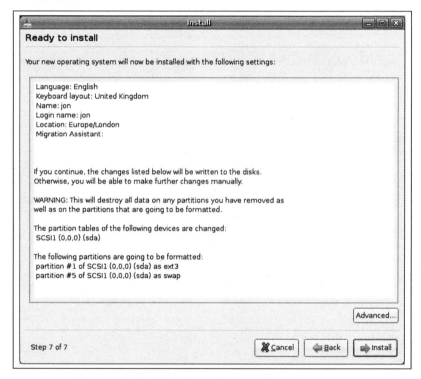

Figure 2-12 Checking the installation options

During the installation, a progress bar will be displayed providing a guide to how long the installation will take, as shown in Figure 2-13.

This may be from 20 minutes to an hour depending on the speed of your system so be patient.

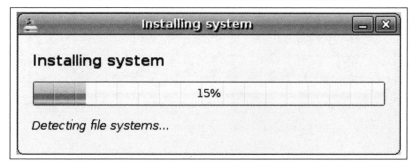

Figure 2-13 Monitoring the progress of the system installation

When the installation is complete, a message will be displayed asking if you wish to continue to use the live CD, or to reboot your system, as shown in Figure 2-14. Click the "Restart now" button.

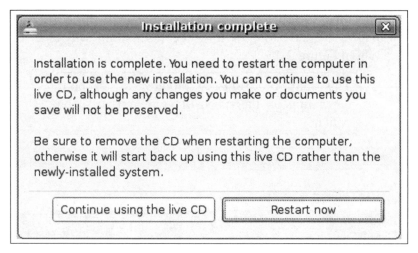

Figure 2-14 The installation is complete

The system will now complete the installation and shutdown; once this is complete a message will be displayed to remove the CD from the CD-Rom drive. Once you have removed the CD, press the enter or return key to restart your computer.

Summary

In this chapter you have taken Ubuntu for a test to make sure it will work correctly on your computer, before committing to installing it onto your hard drive. You are now ready to reboot the system and delve into your new desktop environment.

3
Discovering the Desktop

We are now ready to try out Ubuntu. This chapter explains some of the key features of your new desktop environment and explains the differences and similarities to Windows.

Once the system has rebooted, the Ubuntu "splash" screen is displayed along with a progress bar to provide a guide to how long the system will take to load. After a short while, the login screen will be displayed, as shown in Figure 3-1.

Figure 3-1 The Ubuntu login screen

The login screen displays an "Options" menu in the left-hand bottom corner, and the system name and the current date and time in the lower right-hand corner.

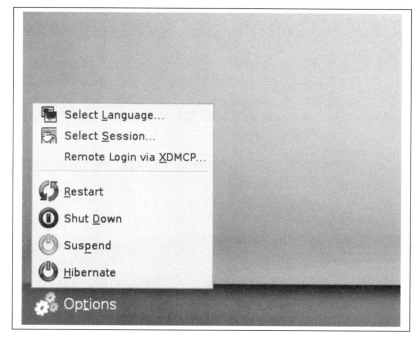

Figure 3-2 The Options menu

The options menu, as shown in Figure 3-2, allows you to put the system to sleep, shut down or restart the computer without having to login. The language can also be changed in multi-lingual environments from this menu. It also allows the user to select a session, this enables you to choose the type of desktop session on login.

For instance, the default desktop environment in Ubuntu Desktop is called GNOME, but its also possible to install the KDE desktop environment (as installed with Kubuntu) and select to login to this desktop rather than GNOME using the "Sessions" option on the "Options" menu.

To login to the system, enter the username that you chose during the installation into the username box and press return. The login box will now change to a password box; enter the password and press return to login.

The desktop in Ubuntu is called GNOME, a popular UNIX and Linux desktop environment. It is based around a menu bar or "top edge panel" along the top of the screen, and a taskbar or "bottom edge panel" along the bottom, as you can see in Figure 3-3.

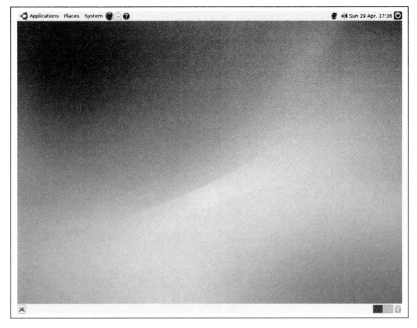

Figure 3-3 The Ubuntu Desktop

The menu bar has three menus on the left-hand side:

- Applications
- Places
- System.

The Applications Menu

The Applications menu lists all the GNOME based applications within sub menus, as shown in Figure 3-4.

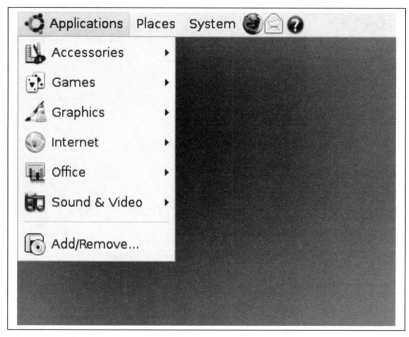

Figure 3-4 Applications Menu

These sub menus include utilities, games, office applications, multimedia applications and image editing applications. The applications are described in detail in the chapters that follow, and the sub menus are:

- Accessories – Useful utilities and tools

- Games – Fun games to use some spare time

- Graphics – Image editing applications

- Internet – Internet and communication applications

- Office – The OpenOffice application suite

- Sound & Vision – Multimedia applications

- Add/Remove - The application package management utility.

The Places Menu

The Places menu lists options that enable you to navigate your documents, connect to other systems or load CD or DVD discs, as shown in Figure 3-5.

Figure 3-5 The Places menu

This menu includes the following applications and short cuts and also includes a sub menu with short cuts to the most recently used documents:

- Home Folder – A short cut to open a file browser in your main folder used for storing files

- Desktop – A short cut to open a file browser showing the desktop

- Computer – A short cut to open a file browser showing the removable and hard disc drives

- CD/DVD Creator – Utility for creating CD or DVD discs

- Network – A short cut to open a file browser showing your network

- Connect to server - Allows you to make network connections to servers for file transfers

- Search for files - A utility for finding files

- Recent documents – A sub-menu with short cuts to your most recently used documents.

The System Menu

Finally, the System menu includes sub-menus for tools for configuring your system, short cuts for on-line help and to shut down the system, as shown in Figure 3-6.

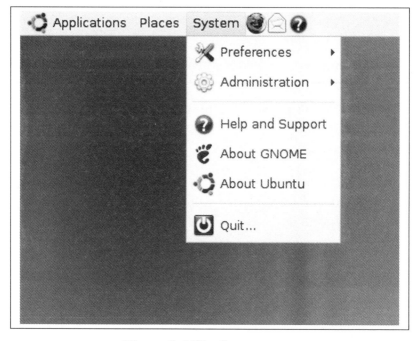

Figure 3-6 The System menu

It contains the following:

- Preferences – A collection of tools for customising your system

- Administration – A collection of administration utilities

- Help and support – The on-line Ubuntu Help Centre

- About GNOME – Information about the GNOME desktop

- About Ubuntu – Information about the Ubuntu Operating System

- Quit… - To logoff, switch users, lock the screen or power down the computer.

The Preferences sub-menu contains utilities for customising your system and its desktop. These contain tools for modifying settings for items like the mouse and keyboard, enabling a screen saver or customising your desktop background and colours. The administration sub-menu lists utilities for maintaining your system, such as configuring the language, creating new user accounts and configuring system updates.

Menu Bar Icons

Next to the System Menu, there are three icons (also shown in Figure 3-6). These icons are:

- Firefox – An icon to start the "Firefox" web browser

- Evolution – An icon to start the "Evolution" email and calendar application

- Help – An icon for the on-line Ubuntu Help Centre.

Notification Area

On the far right-hand side of the top panel, is an area called the "Notification Area". This area shows icons for applications or utilities that might require attention, as shown in Figure 3-7.

For instance, when Ubuntu detects that there are new security updates to install, an icon will appear in this area to inform you. Clicking on this icon will then launch the Update Manager.

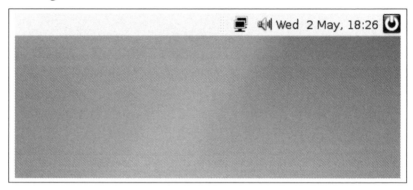

Figure 3-7 Notification Area

This area will normally display:

- Network Manager – an Icon to launch the Network Manager Applet used to configure the network card

- Sound – A short cut to quickly adjust the volume

- Date and Time – The date and time

- Shutdown – An icon to allow you to shut down, reboot or logoff the computer.

Clicking on the items in the notification area may bring up a menu or an option list. For example, left-clicking on the Network Manager icon will display a sub menu to allow you to enable/disable the network card, or to launch the Network Manager applet to manually configure the network card, or to connect to a wireless network. While clicking on the sound icon allows you to adjust the volume. Try clicking on the icons to investigate what options are available.

Editing the Menu Bar

It is possible to edit the menu bar by adding or removing items as required. To remove an item, simply "right-click" the mouse while the cursor is over an icon or menu. This will display a menu to allow you to change the properties of a menu or icon, or to remove the item completely.

Ensure that you really want to delete an item!

If you right-click on a blank section of the menu, a window will be displayed allowing you to add additional items to the bar, or add items back if you have deleted them by mistake. These items include adding your own menus, or utilities to display the weather or stock quotes. Try adding some items, then right-click the item to set any options.

Figure 3-8 Add to Panel

Bottom Panel

The panel along the bottom of the screen includes an icon on the far left-hand side to maximise hidden windows. On the right-hand side it includes an icon which allow you to switch between "workspaces". A workspace is a separate desktop view which allows you to have different windows open and quickly switch between them by clicking on each of the workspace icons. On the far left side is a "wastebasket" icon.

This will open a file browser showing the deleted items. When you select a file or folder and press the delete key, or select the "Move to delete items folder" option from a menu, the item is not permanently deleted but is simply moved to the delete items folder. To really delete items, right-click the "wastebasket" icon and select "Empty the wastebasket" from the menu.

The bottom panel will also display a list of the windows that are open at any time. When a window is minimised it can be restored by clicking on the window title in the bottom panel.

Managing Files

Ubuntu uses the "File Browser" (sometimes called Nautilus) for you to organise and find directories and files, as shown in Figure 3-9. The File Browser can be launched from the "Home Folder" short cut on the "Places" menu. This will open the File Browser focused on your "Home" directory, this is your personal directory used to securely store all your files. The directory is located in the "/Home" directory and is named the same as your user name. If there are multiple users on the same Ubuntu computer, each user will have their own dedicated home directory that only they have permission to access.

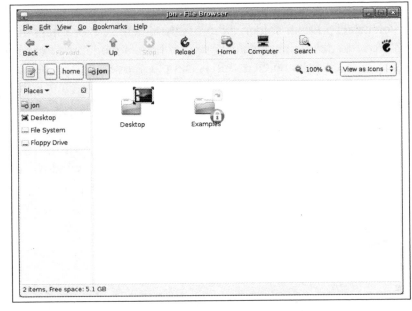

Figure 3-9 The File Browser

The File Browser contains a menu bar allowing you to create new files and directories, or to create "Bookmarks" or short cuts to other directories. It's easy to navigate up and down through different directories by double-clicking the folders to navigate down, and using the "Up" button on the tool bar to navigate back up through the directory tree.

Under the tool bar is the "Location Bar". This bar contains buttons for each folder in a directory tree, so you can also quickly jump to a directory by clicking the button in the bar.

Down the left-hand side of the File Browser is the "Side Pane". This pane contains different information depending on what option is chosen from the pop-up menu on the top of the pane. This menu contains the following options:

- Places – Lists removable media and your home directory

- Information – Displays file and folder information as you select them in the file browser

- Tree – Lists a directory tree as an alternative way of navigating your directory structure

- History – Lists the directories you have been to

- Notes – Allows you to type notes which are displayed when you return to the directory

- Emblems – Tags which can be dragged and dropped on files or directories.

Files and directories can be moved and deleted in a similar manner to other operating systems by dragging or dropping them. Or copied by right-clicking the file and selecting "Copy" or by selecting "Copy" from the "Edit" menu. Files and directories can also be deleted by dragging them to the Waste Basket or selecting "Move to the Deleted items folder" from the "Edit" menu or even right-clicking the file and selecting "Move to the Deleted items folder". Files and directories are only permanently deleted when you choose to "Empty the Wastebasket" from the Waste Basket icon on the bottom panel.

Using Removable Media

When you insert removable media, such as a USB memory stick or blank CD, or DVD disc, Ubuntu will place an icon for the media on your desktop and also on the "Places" menu, as shown in Figure 3-10.

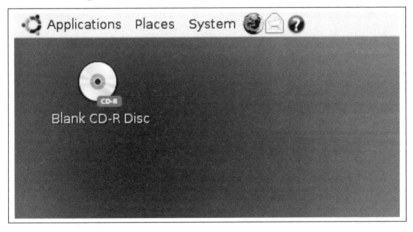

Figure 3-10 Blank CD-R Media

Files and directories can easily be copied by dragging or dropping them from the media to your home directory, or from your home directory to the removable media. If copying files to a USB flash memory device, its important to right-click the icon of the USB memory stick on the desktop and select

"Eject" from the menu. This will write all the information to the memory stick and allow you to safely remove it from the computer. If you simply remove it without selecting "Eject", the data will have not been written to the memory.

Similarly, with blank CD or DVD discs, once you have copied files to the disc, you must double-click the icon of the disc and select "Write to disc" from the "File" menu, as shown in Figure 3-11. Again, this will write the data to disc and allow you to remove it from the computer. Simply removing it from the drive without choosing "Write to disc" will not copy the data.

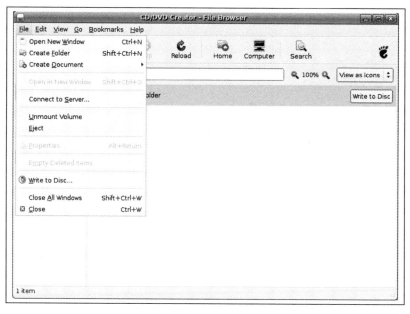

Figure 3-11 Write to Disc

Summary

You should now have familiarised yourself with the GNOME desktop environment and recognised that the system is not too dissimilar to the Windows or Mac OS X systems to use. With what you have learned in this chapter, you should now be ready to copy your work backups from removable media (either USB disc, flash memory or CD or DVD) into your home directory.

4

Configuration

We are now ready to configure your system so that you can connect to a network, set up your printer and create some additional users accounts. Once you have completed this chapter, your computer will be ready to use.

Configuring Network Settings

If your computer is connected to a wired network and your network settings are configured automatically by Dynamic Host Configuration Protocol (DHCP), your network connection will work without you having to configure any of the settings. You can safely skip the following instructions and go on to check for system updates later in this chapter.

However, if you are using a wired network and your router or network is not configured for DHCP, or you are using a wireless network card, it will be necessary to configure them manually. The following sections guide you through the configuration steps.

Wired Network

In order to configure the network, left-click the mouse pointer over the computer icon in the notification bar and select "Manual Configuration" in the pop-up menu. You will be prompted to enter your password, as shown in Figure 4-1.

Ubuntu will prompt for your password whenever an administrative action is performed. This is to ensure that you are performing the action and it is not being performed by any malware which is trying to compromise the security of your system.

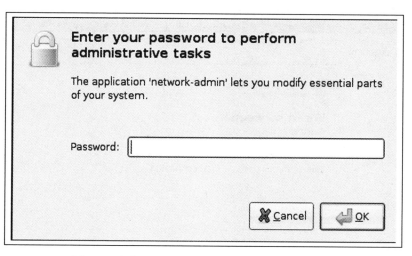

Figure 4-1 Enter your password to perform
administrative tasks

Once your password is entered, the Network Settings utility will be displayed, as shown in Figure 4-2.

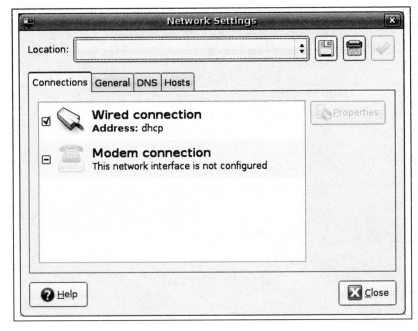

Figure 4-2 Network Settings

With the "Wired Connection" selected, click the "Properties" button.

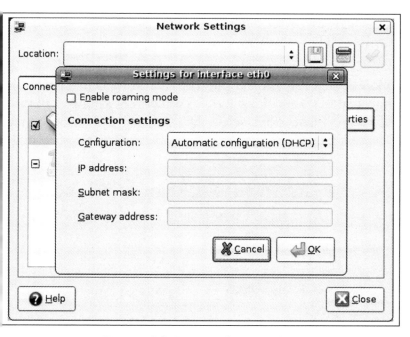

Figure 4-3 Settings for Interface

On the Connections tabs, pull down the "Configuration" menu, as shown in Figure 4-3, and either select "Static IP Address" or "Local Zeroconf network (IPv4 LL)". Choose "Static IP Address" if you want to connect to the Internet through a router and you know the correct address settings. Alternatively if you are on a small network and there is no Internet connection, you can choose the Local Zeroconf setting and Ubuntu will automatically choose an address in order to communicate with other computers that have also been configured the same way.

To configure the address manually, enter the IP address, subnet mask and gateway address (default gateway or router address) and press "OK". The network settings will then be reconfigured. Next, select the "General" tab and enter the "domain name" for your local network, as shown in Figure 4-4.

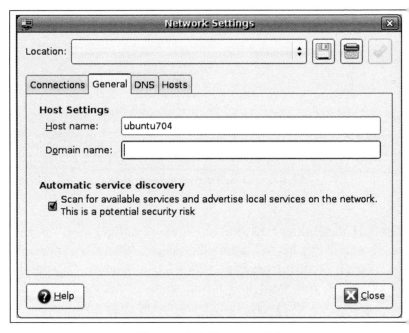

Figure 4-4 General Tab

Then select the "DNS" tab, as shown in Figure 4-5 and enter the IP address of the DNS server for your network by clicking in the "DNS Servers" box and typing the IP address followed by return. If necessary, click the "Add" button to enter another address. You can also configure the local DNS zone to search by clicking the "Add" button and entering the local DNS domain in the "Search Domains" field.

Figure 4-5 DNS Tab

Finally, you can name the configuration by clicking the floppy disc icon and entering a name for the network settings. This is useful if you are using a laptop computer and need to connect to multiple networks that use different network settings. Each configuration can be saved and you can quickly select the correct configuration by selecting it from the "Locations" pull down menu.

Wireless Network

Configuring a wireless network card is very similar to manually configuring a wired network. Left-click the computer icon in the Notification Area to display wireless networks that are available. Then select your wireless network name displayed in the menu. If your network is secured with encryption, you will be prompted to enter the Wireless Network Key.

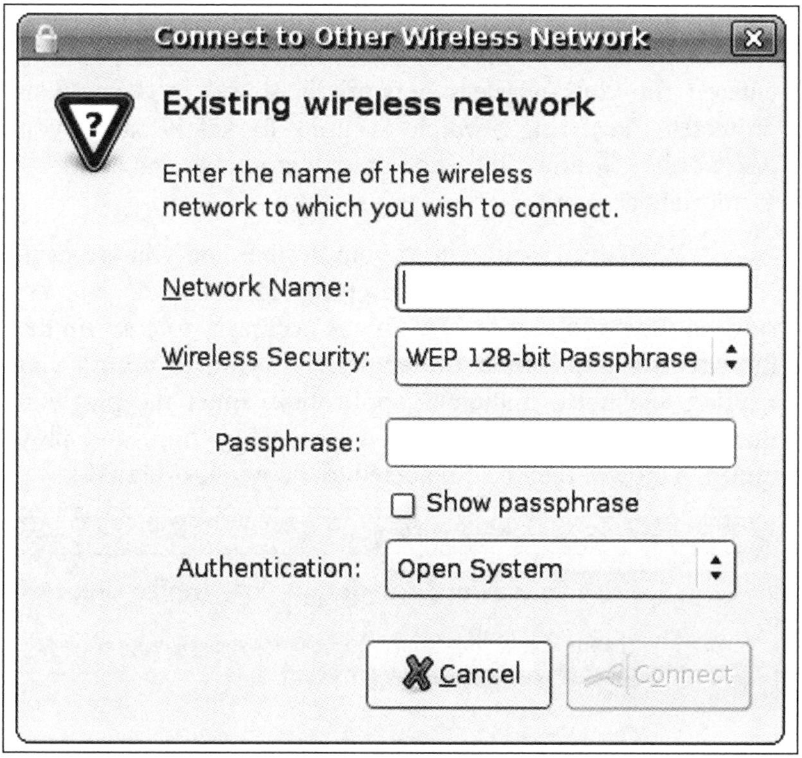

Figure 4-6 Wireless Network Key Required

Select the type of wireless security you are using in the drop-down menu (either a Passphrase, Hex, ASCII or text string) as shown in Figure 4-6, and then enter the key in the text box. Finally, select the authentication method of Open system or Shared key and then click the "Login to Network" button to connect to the wireless network.

During the wireless network set-up you will be prompted to enter a password to give to your "key ring". The password entered for your wireless network is stored in a password protected "key ring" which is used to safely store your passwords. Follow the on-screen prompts and enter a memorial password.

Whenever you login to your system and you are using a wireless network, you will be prompted to unlock your key ring, as shown in Figure 4-7. This is necessary to confirm that the network application (nmapplet) is trying to access your keyring and not a malicious application. Enter the password that you entered when setting up your key ring, and press return. You will then be connected to the wireless network.

Figure 4-7 Unlock keyring

If necessary, you can configure a manual TCP/IP address for your network card in the same way as described in the previous section for a Wired Network. Simply select the "Manual Configuration" setting from the network menu and follow the instructions detailed in the previous section.

Manually Checking for System Updates

Ubuntu is configured to automatically detect when system updates are available and then to ask you if it is convenient for the system to download and install them. An icon will appear in the Notification Area when updates are available and a pop-up message will inform you to click on the icon to install the updates, as can be seen in Figure 4-8.

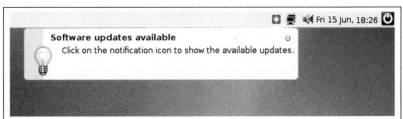

Figure 4-8 System Update Notification

After the system has been installed, and from time to time, it is recommended that you manually check for system updates to ensure the system is kept up to date and that the update mechanism is functioning correctly. To do this, select the "Update Manager" from the "Administration" option on the "System" menu.

Click the "Check" button to start the update. You will be asked to enter your password to perform an administrative function and then the system will connect to the Ubuntu servers and download a list of any updates that might be available. Any updates to install will be displayed in the Update Manager as shown in Figure 4-9.

It is worth spending a few moments scrolling through the list of updates if for no other reason than so you know what is being downloaded and installed.

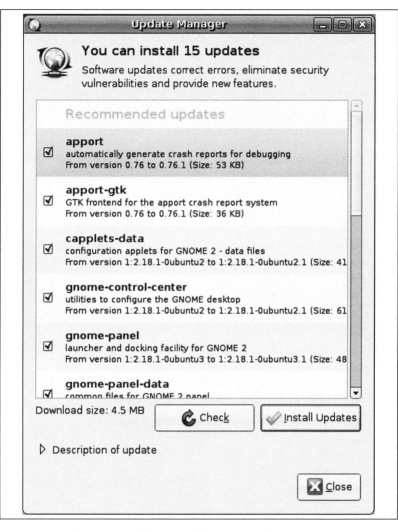

Figure 4–9 Update Manager with updates

Click on the "Install Updates" button to download the recommended updates and complete the installation. When all the updates have been applied, a message will be shown confirming the installation. Click the close button to close the message and then close the Update Manager. If necessary, the system may prompt you to restart your computer in order for the software updates to be completed, as shown in Figure 4-10.

Click on the icon in the notification bar and confirm that you will restart now or later.

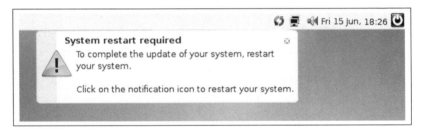

Figure 4-10 System Restart Required

Configuring Printer Settings

The printers utility can be launched from the "Administration" sub-menu from the "System" menu, and allows you to install printers and configure their settings.

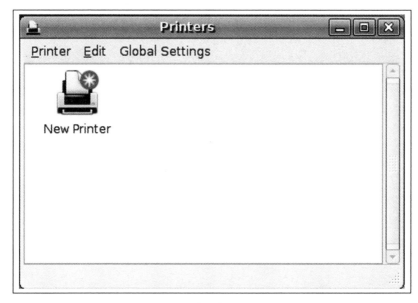

Figure 4-11 Printers

To install a printer, make sure the printer is connected to your computer and switched on, then double-click the "New Printer" icon in the printers utility, as shown in Figure 4-11. The system will then search for the correct printer driver for your printer. Once the printer has been recognised the "Add a Printer" wizard will automatically open.

Figure 4-12 Add a Printer (Printer Type)

Ensure the correct printer is recognised and the settings for local or network connected printer are correct, as shown in Figure 4-12, (change the settings if they are not) and then click the "Forward" button.

Select the most appropriate driver from the list and then click "Forward", name the printer and add a description and location comment if required. Finally, click the "Apply" button to install the printer driver. Your printer will now be displayed in the Printers window.

You can change the properties of the printer by clicking the printer and selecting "Properties" from the "Edit" menu. This will open the properties window, allowing you to set the default printer resolution, page size and orientation, as shown in Figure 4-13. Click the "Print Test Page" button to verify that the printer is working correctly.

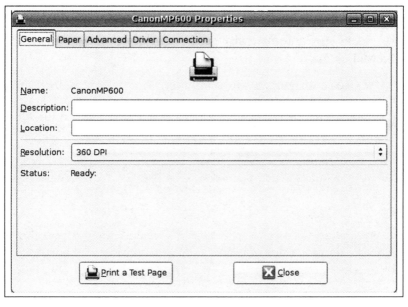

Figure 4-13 Printer Properties

Configuring Time and Date

If your computer is connected to the Internet, it is possible to configure Ubuntu to automatically set the correct time and date on your computer by checking the time against servers on the Internet. These are servers which are configured to check their time against atomic clocks. They then share this accurate time information amongst other servers and client computers using the Network Time Protocol (NTP). This is a standard protocol used by different computer operating systems in order for them to automatically and accurately maintain their internal clocks.

To configure your computer to do this, select the "Time and Date" utility under the "Administration" menu option from the "System" menu.

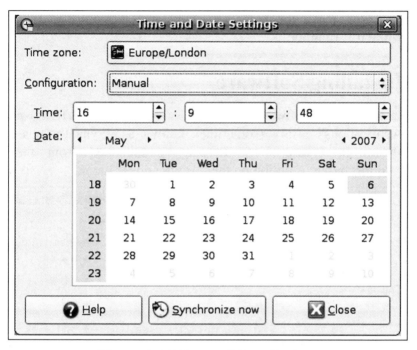

Figure 4-14 Time and Date Settings

Select the "Keep Synchronized with Internet servers" from the Configuration drop-down menu. You will then be prompted to confirm the installation of the NTP software. Click "Install NTP support" to install the software and confirm the on-screen messages to complete the installation.

Once the NTP support is installed you will be returned to the Time and Date utility and the "Keep Synchronized with Internet servers" option will now be selected. Then close the applet and restart the computer, the time will automatically be corrected when the computer starts and at regular periods while it is running.

Installing Software

Installing free software is made easy with the "Add/Remove Applications" utility (sometimes known as "Synaptic"), as shown in Figure 4-15. It can be launched from the "Add/Remove..." option on the "Applications" menu.

Figure 4-15 Add/Remove Applications

Clicking on the "Preferences" button allows you to configure what sources Ubuntu will install software from. Ubuntu uses the following terms for difference software sources:

- Main – Canonical Ltd Supported Open Source software

- Universe – Ubuntu community supported Open Source software

- Restricted – Proprietary drivers

- Multiverse – Copyrighted, although often free, software

- Source Code – Code used during software development.

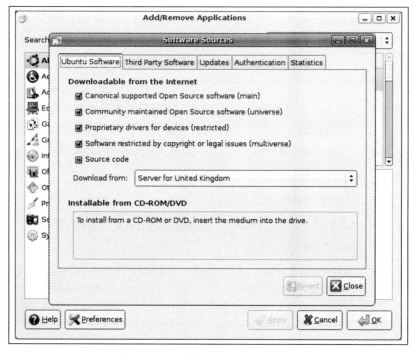

Figure 4-16 Software Sources

Its recommended that for the widest range of software that all the check boxes are ticked except for the "Source Code" option, as shown in Figure 4-16. Ubuntu uses these sources to search for available and compatible software before displaying the options in the Add/Remove Applications utility.

To install software, either browse or search the software by typing in the search box and pressing return. We shall now install the "Java" software which is often required for web sites. This software is not installed by default because it is copyrighted but is still free to use.

Make sure you are connected to the Internet and type "Java" into the search box and press return. A list of the Java software will now be returned in the applications pane. Click the checkbox next to the "Sun Java 6 Web Start". For software that is not supported, or is copyrighted, you will be asked to confirm the installation of unsupported software, click the "Install" button. Then click "OK" and you will be prompted to confirm the installation, as shown in Figure 4-17.

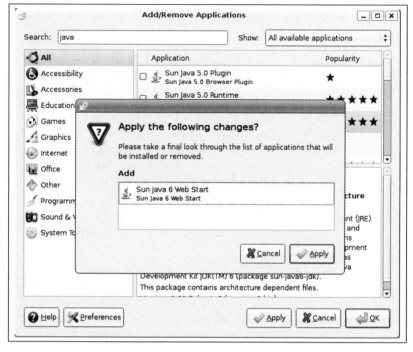

Figure 4-17 Apply the following changes

Once you click "Apply", the Java package will now be downloaded automatically and the installation will commence. During the installation you may be shown some on-screen prompts; follow the instructions to install the software. These prompts will vary depending on the application being installed. You can monitor the progress of the installation as shown in Figure 4-18.

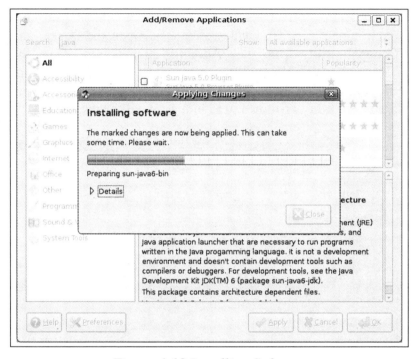

Figure 4-18 Installing Software

When the installation is complete, click the "Close" button on the message informing you that the installation was successful. You will now be able to use Java based web sites.

Creating New Users

Finally, you may need to create additional user accounts for family or colleagues. These allow each user to store their information privately, and configure their desktop environment for their own preferences. Open the "Users and Groups" utility from the "Administration" option from the "System" menu. You will be prompted to enter your password to confirm the administrative task and then the "Users Settings" utility as shown in Figure 4-19 will be displayed.

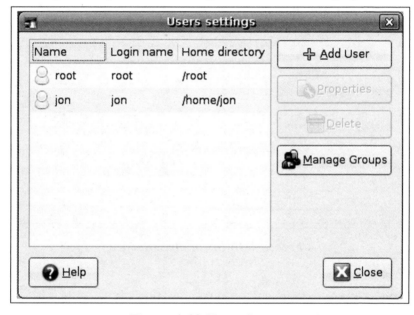

Figure 4-19 Users Settings

Simply click the "Add User" button to start to create a new user account, and the "New User Account" form will be displayed as shown in Figure 4-20.

Figure 4-20 New User Account

Fill out the details on the form and select the type of user to be created from the "Profile" option. Select either "Administrator" for a user who can administrate and change the computer settings, or "Desktop User" for a normal user account who can use the computer but not change its configuration. Click "OK" when you have completed filling in the options and then close the utility.

Restricted Drivers

Ubuntu does not install copyrighted or unsupported software or drivers during the installation. You might therefore discover that some features of your system are not fully configured after the installation. For instance you might find that Ubuntu does not include 3D acceleration for graphics or support certain encryption standards on wireless network cards. However, Ubuntu makes it easy to enable these features using proprietary drivers using the "Restricted Drivers Manager" utility from the "Administration" sub-menu of the "System" menu.

Figure 4-21 Restricted Drivers Manager

If the installation detected that you need to install some additional drivers, they will be listed in the utility and can be installed by simply ticking the check box next to the driver, as can be seen in Figure 4-21. All that you have to do then is confirm the installation and follow any prompts (which may vary depending on what is being installed) to complete the installation. If necessary, you may be prompted to reboot the system to complete the installation and enable the new driver.

Summary

We have now set up your network card, checked for system updates and installed some software. You will now have a fully operational version of Ubuntu. Take a little time to investigate your system, and in the next section of the book we will start to discover the installed applications and configure the system for email and browsing the Internet.

PART 3
Applications

5

Accessories

In this section of the book we will be looking at the applications included with the Ubuntu operating system, and will take you step-by-step, through setting up each of the applications where necessary. This chapter will start by covering the Ubuntu accessories. These are small utilities and applications that can be launched from the "Accessories" sub-menu of the "Applications" menu.

Calculator

As the name suggests, this utility is the built-in calculator. It's launched from the "Calculator" shortcut of the "Accessories" sub-menu.

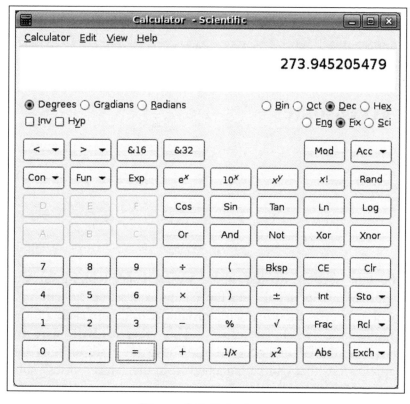

Figure 5-1 Calculator

When launching the utility, it appears that the calculator is a very simple application. However, the display mode is controlled from the "View" menu which enables the calculator to be switched between the following modes:

- Basic

- Advanced

- Financial

- Scientific (as shown in Figure 5-1).

Also controlled from the "View" menu are various useful options such as the ability to show trailing zeros, thousands separator, left-to-right or arithmetic precedence and the memory registers which allow up to 10 numbers to be stored in one of the memory positions.

Character Map

The Character Map application (http://live.gnome.org/Gucharmap), launched from the "Character Map" short cut, is a small application that allows you to browse the characters available in a particular font, and to insert special characters into a text document, as shown in Figure 5-2.

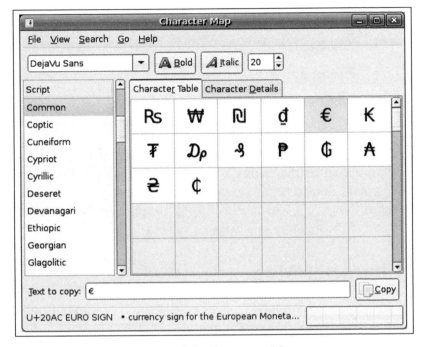

Figure 5-2 Character Map

This allows you to access special characters that may be available in a font but are not shown on your keyboard. These may include special accented characters, mathematical symbols or punctuation marks. As Ubuntu is a multi-language system, Character Map displays characters in all the installed language scripts using the "Unicode" character set. This is a standard character set devised to include all of the characters used in all the world's written languages.

The Character Map window shows a display area which can be changed between showing the characters available in the current script, and a character details tab which shows details of an individual character. When a character or symbol is double-clicked, it is entered into the "Text to copy" text field allowing you to create a text or symbol string that can be copied to another document.

Dictionary

The dictionary utility, started from the "Dictionary" short cut from the "Accessories" sub-menu, is an on-line dictionary utility that allows you to search for words and terms using an Internet dictionary source, as shown in Figure 5-3.

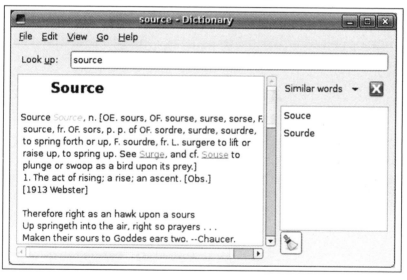

Figure 5-3 Dictionary

Words can be searched in the dictionary by simply typing the word into the "Look up" field and pressing return. The definition will then be displayed in the window below the look up field. As the utility uses an Internet site, "dict.org", as the source it will only work while the system is connected to the Internet.

The "Preferences" option on the "Edit" menu allows the default dictionary server to be modified or a new dictionary source to be added, by clicking the "Add" button and entering the details of the new dictionary server, as can be seen in Figure 5-4.

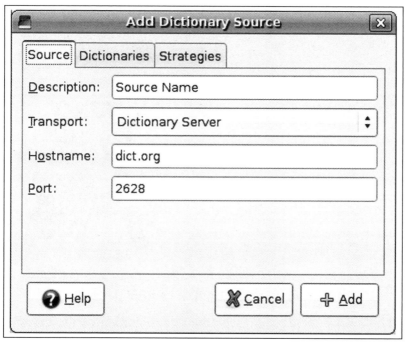

Figure 5-4 Add Dictionary Source

Disk Usage Analyser

A new utility introduced with Ubuntu 7.04 is the "Disk Usage Analyser", which again can be launched from the "Accessories" sub-menu from the short cut with the same name.

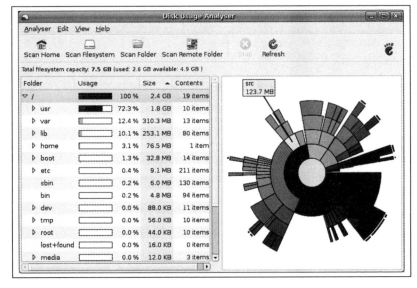

Figure 5-5 Disc Usage Analyser

This utility displays a graphical representation of the current disc usage, as shown in Figure 5-5. The window is split into two sections, with the left-hand pane displaying the directory structure, size and usage in percentage, while the right-hand side shows a graphical representation of the directory structure. The utility can be used to analyse a complete disc or just a local or network directory structure. The menu bar contains buttons which allows scans to be run against the following options, which are also listed under the "Analyser" menu:

- User's home directory
- Entire file system

- A particular local directory

- A remote/network directory.

Clicking on the file system button will start a scan on the entire file system which may take some time. Once the scan is complete, the left-hand pane will display a tree of the directory structure starting at the "root" or "/" directory and listing all directories immediately under the root directory. Each sub-directory is shown with the size, number of contents and the percentage that this directory makes up of the total.

Each directory can be expanded or collapsed by toggling the small triangle next to the directory name. This will cause the sub-directories to be displayed along with their details.

The right-hand pane displays the graphical representation of the statistics from the left-hand pane. The centre of the graphic is the root directory of the scan and fanning out from the centre is each of the subdirectories until the entire directory is shown. The size of each ring or block is in proportion to the size of the directory.

Take Screenshot

This application is a simple utility that allows the entire active desktop or just the active window to be captured and saved as a ".png" or Portable Network Graphics file.

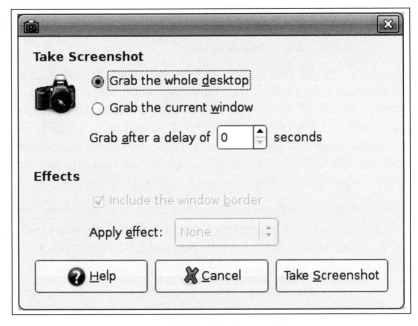

Figure 5-6 Take Screenshot

Simply run the application and select either "Grab the whole desktop" or "Grab the current window" before clicking the "Take screenshot" to take a snapshot of your workspace or active window, as shown in Figure 5-6. Once the snapshot has been taken, the application will prompt you to name and save the screen shot.

Alternatively, you can enter a number of seconds to delay before the picture is taken, this allows you to position the mouse and window in a suitable position before taking the picture.

Terminal

The "Terminal" short cut launches the GNOME terminal window; this allows command line access to the GNU/Linux shell environment.

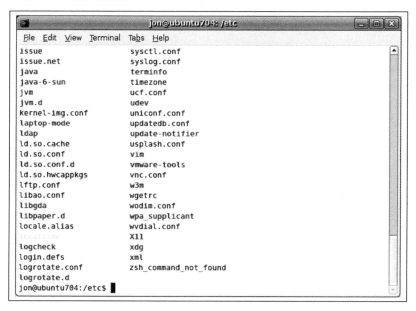

Figure 5-7 Terminal

A "shell" is a program that interprets and executes text commands as they are typed, or run from a text file called a "script".

When the terminal is started, a "terminal window" is displayed containing a "command prompt" where UNIX commands are typed and executed when the return key is pressed, as can be seen in Figure 5-7.

Text Editor

The Text Editor or "Gedit" (http://www.gedit.org) as it is sometimes referred to, is run from the "Text Editor" icon.

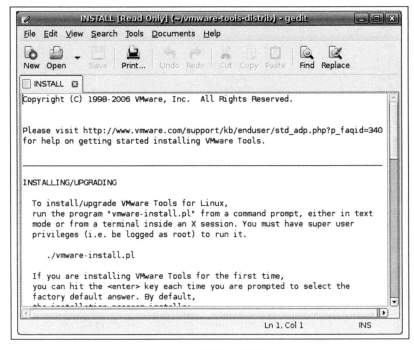

Figure 5-8 Text Editor

This application is a simple and easy to use application for editing text-based files or scripts, as shown in Figure 5-8.

However, behind its ease of use the application has many sophisticated features such as full support for international text, highlighting of syntax in text files and scripts (such as HTML, C, C++, Java, Perl, XML, etc), file reverting, editing of remote files and support for "plug ins" to add additional functionality. These advanced features are in addition to standard text editing features such as undo, redo, cut, copy, paste, spell checking, search, word wrap and line numbering.

Files can be created or opened from the options on the "File" menu, however the text editor also supports "dragging and dropping" of files into the editor window to open files.

In order to configure syntax colouring when editing certain files or scripts, the "Preferences" option on the "Edit" menu allows the highlight mode to changed according to the type of script being edited, as shown in Figure 5-9.

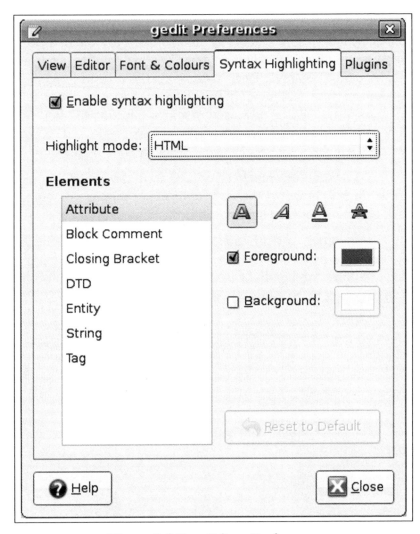

Figure 5-9 Text Editor Preferences

Tomboy Notes

"Tomboy" (http://www.gnome.org/projects/tomboy) is a note taking application that allows notes to be created, managed and stored.

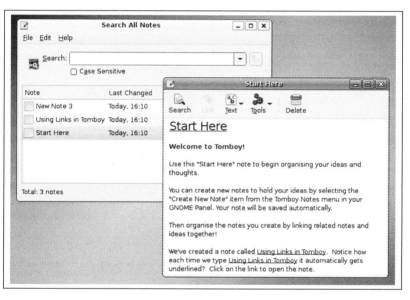

Figure 5-10 Tomboy Notes

When the application is running, it adds a small icon to the Notification Area of the top panel, allowing new notes to be quickly and easily created by selecting "Create New Note" from the drop-down menu from the notification area icon. Alternatively, the application also allows new notes to be created from the "File" menu of the "Search All Notes" window.

Text is simply typed on the new note and can be formatted from the drop-down menu of the "Text" button on the notes tool bar, as shown in Figure 5-10. When the note is closed it is stored along with other notes and can be accessed again from either the drop-down menu or the "Search All Notes" window. Notes are deleted from the "Delete" option on the "Edit" menu.

The application is particularly useful for keeping lots of free-form text that you need to refer to later, but might not be large enough to start a new file or OpenOffice document. Accessing or finding the information at a later date is made easy by the search functionality, enabling information to be quickly retrieved.

Like the Text Editor discussed earlier, Tomboy Notes also supports "plug ins" that allow software developers to easily add functionality to the application. These include "plug ins" which allow notes to be created from the "Evolution" email client, saving the note as a web HTML file and also to see which notes relate to the currently active note. These plug ins can be used from the "Tools" drop-down menu from the tools button.

Summary

In this section, we started to take a look at the numerous applications included with Ubuntu, these ranged from the simple built-in calculator to the sophisticated disc usage analyser. In the next chapter we investigate the Graphics applications in order to manage, create and edit digital images.

6

Graphics

As you we have already discovered, Ubuntu is pre-installed with numerous applications, this chapter will discuss the applications dedicated for graphics. These applications provide the tools required for importing, scanning, managing and editing your photographs and pictures. To launch the individual applications, go to the "Graphics" sub-menu from the "Applications" menu.

F-Spot Photo Manager

F-Spot (http://f-spot.org) is a personal photo manager that allows you to import, organise, print, email, backup and even edit your photographs. When the application is launched for the first time, it will prompt you to import images from either a connected camera or another folder such as a backup DVD.

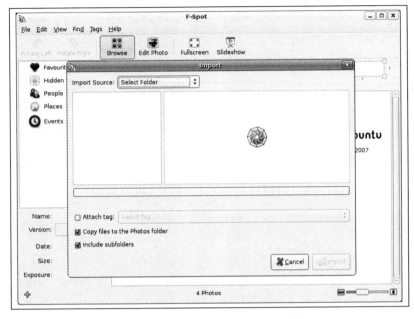

Figure 6-1 F-Spot Import window

Once the source is selected, either a folder, camera or memory card, as shown in Figure 6-1, F-Spot will copy the images into your "photos" folder which is located under your home directory. The program creates a directory structure based upon the creation date of the image, this is made up of the format photos/year/month/date. This allows you to easily recognise the creation date of an image. Once the images have been imported, the F-Spot browse window is opened, this window allows the images to be displayed and tagged.

Figure 6–2 F-Spot Browse window

The browse window contains a bar along the top of the window which can be used to rapidly find photographs by date, as moving the bar scans the photo folder for images of the relevant creation date, as shown in Figure 6-2. Once you have found the images you require, they can be "tagged" with a user-customisable tag to aid finding and categorising your pictures.

The predefined tags are shown in the list on the left hand side of the browse window. To create a new tag, simply right-click with the mouse pointer in the tag pane. To tag a photo, select the images in the image pane and then drag and drop the relevant tag onto one of the photographs, alternatively right-click in the images window and select "Attach Tag". Then, if you double-click the tag, you will be able to search for all photographs with the associated tag.

You can change the view within the browse window by pressing one of the buttons on the tool bar. Pressing the "Edit" button will bring up a comments field at the bottom of the window. This allows you to enter a comment for each image. Also shown below the comments field, is the edit tool bar. Various simple edit functions can be achieved within the F-Spot Manager, these include:

- Change the aspect ratio
- Crop
- Remove red-eye
- Adjust the image's colours
- Convert to black and white
- Convert to sepia
- Rotate the angle of the image to straighten the horizon
- Create a soft focus effect.

Other edit functions are also available from the "Edit" menu, such as the ability to sharpen the image. F-Spot will also allow you to send the image via email, print, or export the image to CD or a web based photo sharing site such as Flickr (http://www.flickr.com) or Picasweb (http://picasaweb.google.com). This is easily achieved from the options on the "File" menu.

GIMP Image Editor

GIMP (http://www.gimp.org) or GNU Image Manipulation Program is a full featured graphics editor, that aims to provide a freely distributed alternative to commercial programs such as Adobe Photoshop. It provides many advanced features for photo retouching, image composition and image creation and can be seen in Figure 6-3.

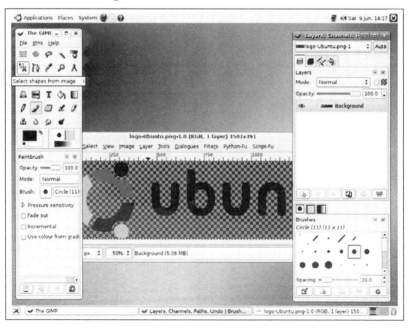

Figure 6-3 The GIMP

GIMP has so many features that to cover it in detail requires a book to itself. Therefore we will just touch some of the many features it has to offer. From the GIMP window, open one of the example images or one of your own digital images by selecting "Open" from the "File" menu from within the GIMP application, and then selecting the relevant file. The image will be opened in its own window, and will be scaled to fit the size of your monitor.

The application is displayed in several panes, the first pane is the main toolbox, and below it are the tool options. This pane contains several tools, for selecting parts of the image, brushes for painting, tools for editing or erasing parts of the image, etc. and can be seen in Figure 6-4.

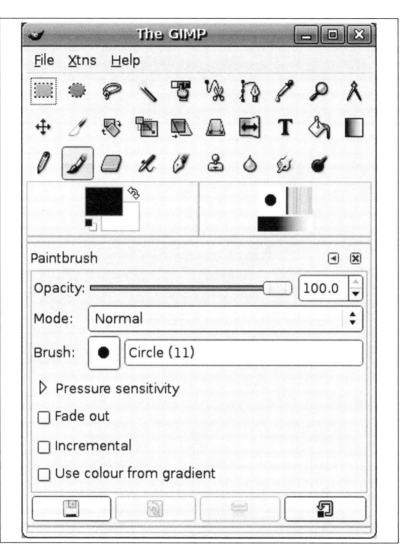

Figure 6-4 GIMP Tool Box

The image being worked on is displayed in its own window with a menu bar for all the file and editing functions, as shown in Figure 6-5. Depending on the performance of your computer, it is possible to have several images open and worked on at the same time. The menu bar options are also available by right-clicking the mouse pointer within the image window.

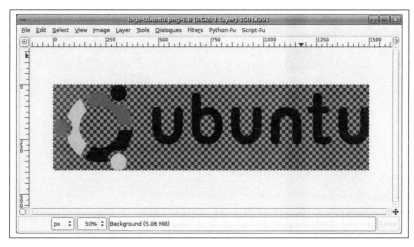

Figure 6-5 GIMP Image window

The final window contains the Layers Dialog, as shown in Figure 6-6. This window is used to apply and edit multiple layers of an image, allowing it to be modified in many different ways. Below the layers dialog, are the brushes, patterns and gradients dialog. These options are used when painting or modifying an image.

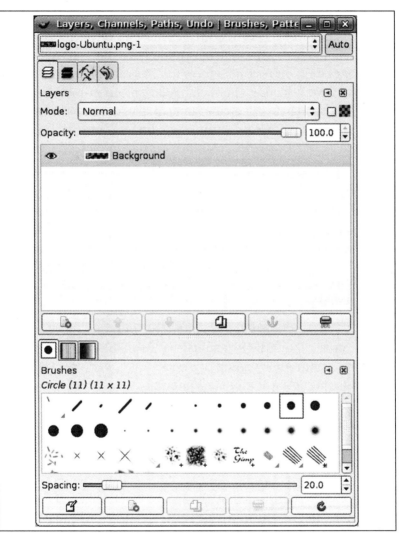

Figure 6-6 GIMP Layers Box

Some simple tasks that you might want to achieve using GIMP is to change the size of the image; this can be easily achieved by selecting the "Scale Image" option from the "Image" menu. Another common task is to crop the image. This can easily be achieved by selecting the rectangular selection tool from the tool palette. Then select the area of the image you want to keep and chose "Crop" from the "Image" menu. This will remove all of the area of the image outside the selection.

If at any time you want to undo your action, this can be achieved by selecting the "Undo" option on the "Edit" menu or using the Ctrl+Z command key combination. Another useful way of undoing an action is from the "Undo History" dialog. Stacked under the "Layers" dialog is the Undo History dialog which contains a history of the actions performed on the image and allows you to jump back to any stage at any time, so undoing multiple actions in one go.

For additional information and tutorials on using the application, the GIMP manual is available at the GIMP website (http://www.gimp.org/docs) as well as detailed tutorials (http://www.gimp.org/tutorials).

gThumb Image Viewer

As the name suggest, gThumb (http://gthumb.sourceforge.net) is a thumbnail image viewer. It performs many of the functions also performed by the F-Spot Photo Manger, such as importing images from a camera, editing, viewing and slide show functions, as shown in Figure 6-7.

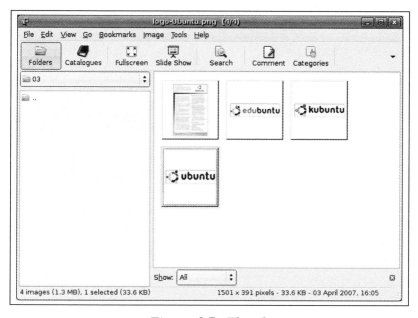

Figure 6-7 gThumb

The main difference between the two applications is that gThumb lacks the tagging of images performed by F-Spot. However, instead gThumb allows the creation of "Libraries" and "Catalogues". These allow images to be collated together in user-created collections. A library allows the grouping of several catalogues which are used to actually group the images.

To create a catalogue, click the "Catalogue" button on the tool bar to switch to the catalogue view. Then right-click in the left-hand pane and select "New Catalogue". Images can be added to a catalogue by simply selecting the image and right-clicking on it. Then selecting the catalogue from the context menu.

Summary

In this chapter we discovered the many open source applications which Ubuntu includes for managing and editing digital photos and graphics files. These applications include the feature-rich GIMP image editing application that offers many of the features provided by commercial photo editing software. In the next chapter we look into the Internet applications and configure them for collecting email, browsing the Web and communicating over the Internet.

7

OpenOffice

In this chapter we discover the OpenOffice.org suite. OpenOffice.org (http://openoffice.org) is a free, but fully-featured suite of office applications for word processing, databases, spreadsheets and presentations. We look at the main applications, see how they compare with other office suites and learn enough to get started using the applications.

Like the Ubuntu community, OpenOffice.org is supported, maintained and developed by the OpenOffice.org community. The suite includes the following applications:

- Base – Database applications
- Calc – Spreadsheet application
- Draw – A vector based drawing program
- Impress – Presentation software

- Math – Mathematical formulae editor
- Writer – Word processing software.

Only the main four applications (Writer, Calc, Impress and Base) are pre-installed on Ubuntu and are available from the "Office" sub-menu of the "Applications" menu.

Base

Base is the database application from the OpenOffice.org suite and is launched from the "OpenOffice.org Database" short-cut from the "Office" sub-menu. The application provides several sophisticated tools for working with databases from an easy to use interface, as shown in Figure 7-1. It allows the creation and editing of forms, reports, and queries, either with a server based database (such as dBASE, MySQL or Oracle) or a local database file (using HSQLDB or Microsoft Access).

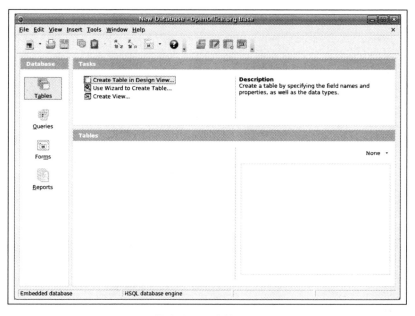

Figure 7-1 OpenOffice.org Base

When launched, Base starts a wizard to step you through either creating a new database or opening an existing file, as shown in Figure 7-2.

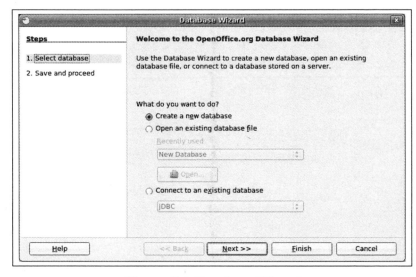

Figure 7-2 Database Wizard

When the wizard is displayed, select the "New Database" option and click the "Next" button. The application will then ask if you wish to register the database and open it, as can be seen in Figure 7-3. Ensure these options are selected and click "Finish". You are then prompted to name the database.

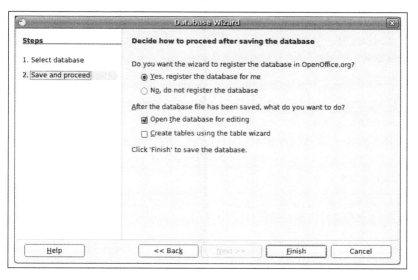

Figure 7-3 Database Wizard

Registering the database allows it to be accessible to the other OpenOffice.org applications such as Writer and Calc. Once the database is created as an OpenOffice.org database file (.odb), the main Base window is displayed where you can create tables, queries, forms and reports. The subject of databases is beyond the scope of this book, so to learn more, OpenOffice.org offers extensive documentation at http://documentation.openoffice.org/manuals/index.html.

Calc

OpenOffice.org Calc has numerous analysis, charting and decision-making features with over 300 functions for statistical, financial and mathematical operations. Calc also includes a Scenario Manager allowing "what if" analysis, and enables the generation of 2-D and 3-D charts which can be integrated into other OpenOffice.org documents.

Like the other applications, Calc will open and use Microsoft Excel workbooks or export spreadsheets to Adobe's Acrobat (.pdf) or the Internet's Hyper Text Markup (.html) standards. The application can be launched from the "OpenOffice.org Spreadsheet" shortcut on the "Office" sub-menu and can be seen in Figure 7-4.

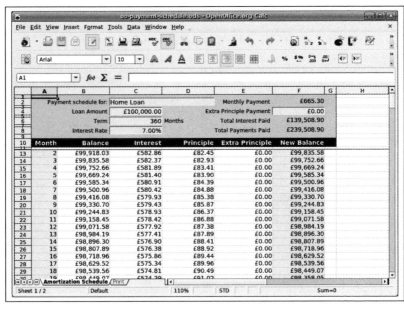

Figure 7-4 OpenOffice.org Calc

As can be seen in Figure 7-4, Calc resembles many other spreadsheet applications with the standard and formatting tool bars, a formula bar and column and row headers. Along the bottom of window, below the cells, are the "sheet" tabs. These allows multiple work sheets to be created within the same document. Moving between sheets is achieved by simply clicking on the relevant tab. Working with Calc files is the same as other applications with the standard "Open" or "Save" options from the file menu. Calc defaults to using its own OpenOffice file formats, as shown in Table 7-1:

Type	Format Extension
Spreadsheet	.ods
Spreadsheet Template	.odt

Table 7-1 OpenOffice.org Calc File Formats

However, in addition to the standard Calc formats, it also allows the opening of many different spreadsheet types as shown in Table 7-2:

Spreadsheet Type	Format Extension
Data Interchange Format	.dif
dBase	.dbf
HyperText Markup Language	.htm and .html files
Lotus 1-2-3	.wk1, .wks, and .123
Microsoft Excel 2003 XML	.xml
Microsoft Excel 4.x–5.0/95	.xls, .xlw, and .xlt
Microsoft Excel 97/2000/XP	.xls, .xlw, and .xlt
OpenOffice.org 1.x	.sxc and .stc
Pocket Excel	.pxl
Quattro Pro 6.0	.wb2
Rich Text Format	.rtf
StarCalc formats	.sdc and .vor
SYLK	.slk
Text	.csv and .txt

Table 7-2 Calc Spreadsheet Formats

Spreadsheets in Calc can be exported to many of these formats by either choosing "Save as" from the file menu, using the "Export to PDF" option, or by exporting the file via email using the "Send" option on the "File" menu.

Impress

OpenOffice.org Impress is the presentation application of the suite, and provides a multimedia tool enabling presentations to be created with animation, effects, sounds and video. It is launched from the "OpenOffice.org Presentation" short cut.

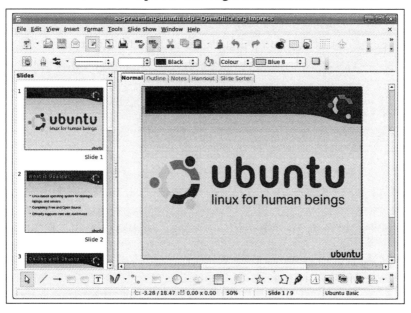

Figure 7-5 OpenOffice.org Impress

The Impress interface is very similar to other slide show based presentation software, as shown in Figure 7-5, and is very easy to get started. It defaults to saving files in the native OpenOffice.org file formats as shown below in Table 7-3:

Type	Format Extension
Presentation	.odp
Presentation Template	.otp

Table 7-3 OpenOffice.org Impress File Formats

However, it can also open and convert presentations from many other commercial applications as shown in Table 7-4:

Presentation Type	Format Extension
Microsoft PowerPoint 97/2000/XP	.ppt, .pps, and .pot
OpenOffice.org 1.x	.sxi and .sti
StarDraw and StarImpress	.sda, .sdd, .sdp, and .vor
CGM – Computer Graphics Metafile	.cgm

Table 7-4 Impress Presentation Formats

When launched, the application will open the new presentation wizard, as shown in Figure 7-6.

> If you don't want to be prompted with this wizard each time you start the application or create a new file, simply tick the "Do Not Show This Wizard Next Time" check box.

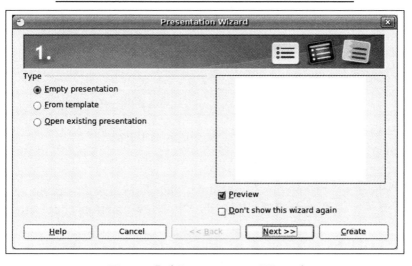

Figure 7-6 Presentation Wizard

The wizard provides the option to either create a new empty presentation, to open a template, or open an existing file. Select the option to create a blank presentation and click "Next".

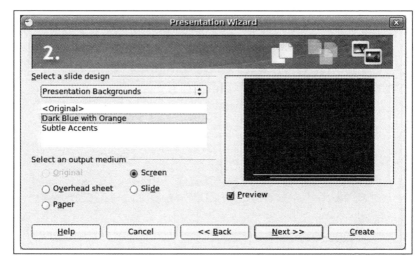

Figure 7-7 Presentation Wizard

Select a presentation type under the slide design option, as shown in Figure 7-7. With the "Preview" option checked, a preview of the slide will appear in the wizard when you choose the slide design. The output medium option will optimise the presentation for the type of media being used, select "Screen" and click the "Next" button.

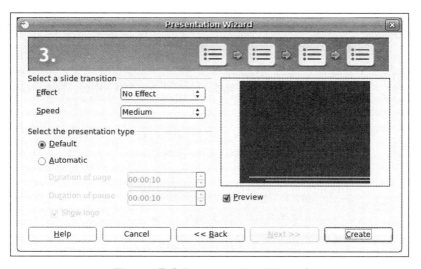

Figure 7-8 Presentation Wizard

When you select a sideshow to be displayed on the screen, the final wizard screen allows you to choose an effect for the transition between each slide, as shown in Figure 7-8. Click "Create" to create your blank presentation once you have made your selection.

The Impress window is split into three main sections, the slides pane on the left-hand side contains thumbnails of the slides in your presentation. This pane allows you to organise, delete, rename or copy the individual slides. In the middle of the window is the workspace, this has five tabs along the top of the pane. These tabs allow you to change the view of the workspace:

- Normal view is used to format and design an individual slide

- Outline view shows the topics and lists of each slide in an outline format and is used to edit titles, headings and topics

- Notes view allows presentation notes to be added to each slide, these are hidden from the actual presentation view

- Slide sorter view shows thumbnails of each slide and is used to rearrange the order or add transitions between selected slides

- Handout view enables the printing of slides for a handout.

The task pane is also split into the following sections:

- Master pages is used to define the slide style to be used for the presentation

- Layout allows the selection of one of 20 standard layouts to be selected for each individual slide

- Custom Animation enables the selection of animations to be applied to a selected element of an individual slide

- Slide transition enables you to choose out of 56 transitions to be applied between slides.

When you have completed your presentation, it can be saved as an OpenOffice.org file, or one of the many proprietary file formats. However, Impress also allows files to be exported as Adobe Acrobat (.pdf), HyperText Markup Language (.html) or even a Macromedia Flash (.swf) animation by selecting "Export" from the "File" menu.

Writer

OpenOffice.org Writer is available from the "OpenOffice.org Word Processor" short cut on the "Office" sub-menu. Writer is a fully-featured word processing application that offers many of the features of commercial applications such as Microsoft Word, and allows the creation of letters, brochures, reports and documents, as shown in Figure 7-9. If you are familiar with Word or WordPerfect applications you will instantly be very familiar with Writer.

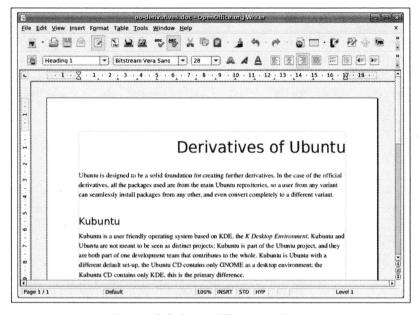

Figure 7-9 OpenOffice.org Writer

The Writer application looks very similar to any other word processing application, with the familiar tool bars shown along the top of the window under the menu bar. Working with files is simple with the standard "Open" or "Save" options from the file menu. Writer defaults to using its own OpenOffice file formats which are as shown below in Table 7-5:

Type	Format Extension
Text Document	.odt
Text Template	.ott
Text Master document	.odm

Table 7-5 OpenOffice File Formats

Its important to remember that if you share documents with users of other word processing software such as Microsoft Word, they may not be able to open the OpenOffice default file formats. However, Writer is capable of saving to proprietary formats such as Microsoft Word (.doc) or standard formats such as Rich Text Format (.rtf), HyperText Markup Language (.html) and Extensible Markup Language (.xml). The full listed of supported files are shown in the listed below in Table 7-6:

Type	Format Extension
AportisDoc (Palm)	.pdb
DocBook	.xml
HTML Document (OpenOffice.org Writer)	.html and .htm
Microsoft Word 2003 XML	.xml
Microsoft Word 6.0, 95, and 97/2000/XP	.doc
OpenOffice.org 1.x Text Document Template	.stw
OpenOffice.org 1.x Text Document	.sxw
Pocket Word	.psw
Rich Text Format	.rtf
StarWriter 3.0, 4.0, and 5.0	.sdw
StarWriter 3.0, 4.0, and 5.0 Template	.vor
Text and Text Encoded	.txt

Table 7-6 Supported File Formats

A document can be exported as one of these formats by choosing "Save as..." from the "File" menu. Alternatively, if you often exchange files with users using a different application, you can configure Writer to default to one of these standard file formats by selection "Options..." from the "Tools" menu, as shown in Figure 7-10. The default file options are listed under "General" under the "Load/Save" section of the preferences.

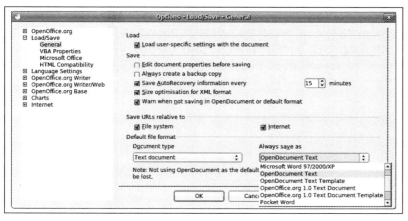

Figure 7-10 Writer Options

One of the many useful features that is not supported by many word processing applications is the ability to directly export as an Adobe Acrobat (.pdf) file, this can be achieved from the "Export as PDF..." option on the "File" menu. Writer will also connect to your email client to send a document directly by email from within the Writer application by choosing one of the options under the "Send" sub-menu on the "File" menu.

Summary

OpenOffice.org provides a full-feature suite of applications for all your day to day office computing tasks. As we have discovered, it can be used to open and interoperate with many of the commercial applications and even offers features not provided by some such as exporting as Adobe Acrobat format. As the OpenOffice.org suite warrants an entire book to cover its extensive features, for a full list of features, documentation and tutorials for all of the OpenOffice.org applications, refer to the extensive documentation provided by the OpenOffice.org community at http://documentation.openoffice.org/.

8

Internet

This chapter will discuss the Internet applications included with Ubuntu, and will take you through, step-by-step, how to configure the applications to browse the Web, read and send emails, chat on-line and make free voice calls over the broadband. All these applications can be found under the "Internet" sub-menu of the "Applications" menu.

Ekiga Softphone

Ekiga (http://www.gnomemeeting.org) is an open source voice and video conferencing application which was previously called "GnomeMeeting". It can be run on various versions of GNU/Linux as well as Windows operating systems, and inter-operates with other similar applications which are based on industry standard protocols such as Windows Messenger, IP

Phones, Gizmo Project and NetMeeting. It does not operate with proprietary applications such as Skype as they are not based on an open protocol.

Setup

Setting up the application is made easy by a wizard that will automatically step you through the process to create an account so that other people will be able to contact you. When the application is launched for the first time, the configuration wizard will be shown as shown in Figure 8-1.

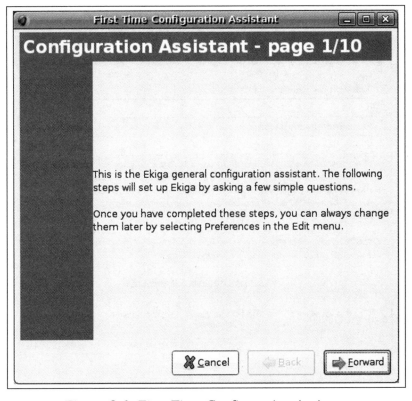

Figure 8-1 First Time Configuration Assistant

Click the "Forward" button to start the configuration process. On the first screen simply enter your name and click "Forward", as shown in Figure 8-2. The next screen will prompt you to enter details of an existing SIP account, or to create an account if you do not already have one.

Figure 8-2 ekiga.net Account

A SIP account allows other people to find you and make voice calls to your computer. If you already have a SIP account from another application, you can enter the account and password on this screen and click "Forward". If you have never used a Voice Over IP (VOIP) application before, click on the "Get an ekiga.net SIP account" hyperlink to create a new account, or alternatively go to the http://www.ekiga.net web site. On the web site, click the "Subscribe" link and complete the form to create a SIP account, as shown in Figure 8-3.

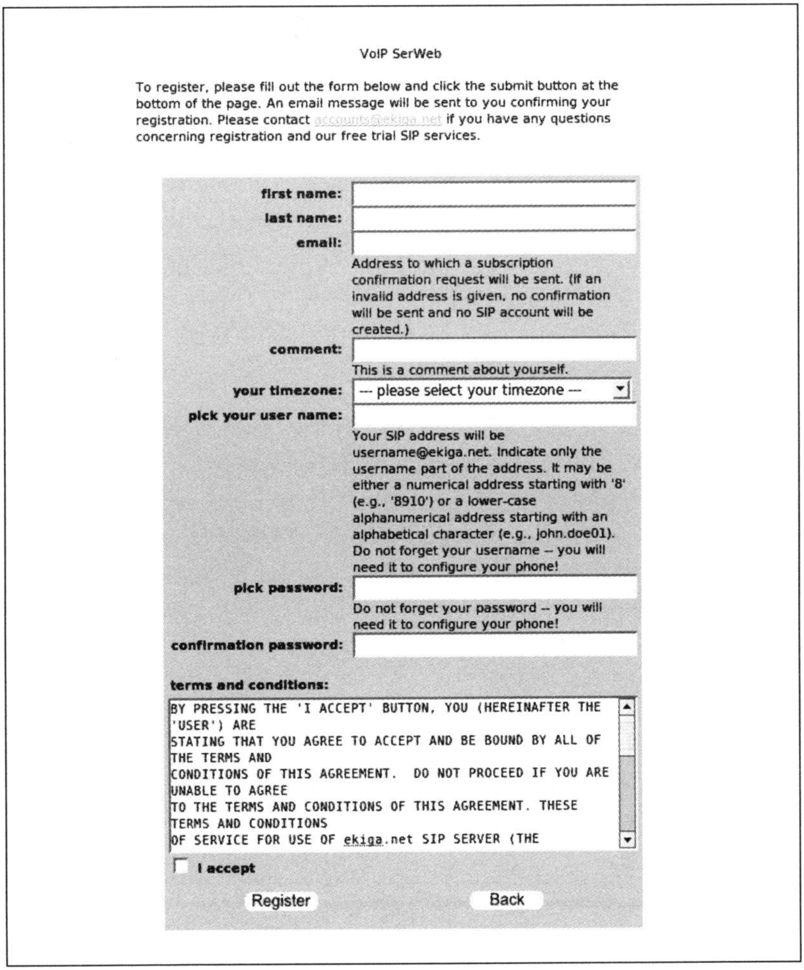

Figure 8-3 ekiga.net registration

Once you have created an Ekiga SIP account, or using the details of existing account, enter the account name and password into the wizard and click "Forward". You will then be asked how you are connected to the Internet, this allows the application to optimise its quality settings to make the best use of your Internet connection. Select your Internet connection type, either "56K Modem" for a dial-up connection (or "narrow band"), "ISDN", "xDSL/Cable" for an ADSL or Cable modem connection (or "broadband"), or "T1/LAN" for a direct connection to the Internet. When you click "Forward" the wizard will automatically determine how your Internet connection is made and will configure itself for the most appropriate connection.

Confirm the recommendations made by Ekiga and click "Forward" in the wizard. The application then checks how your sound system works on Ubuntu and will ask you to confirm its selection for the Audio Manager, as shown in Figure 8-4. Again Ekiga should make the correct selection so click "Forward" to confirm its choice. It will then ask you to confirm the Audio Devices it has detected.

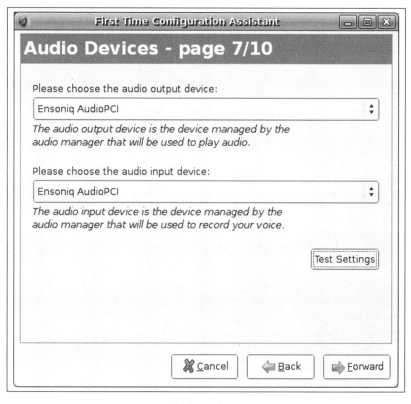

Figure 8-4 Audio Devices

Press the "Test" button to try recording a short message and Ekiga will play back the recording to confirm your audio is working correctly. Click "OK" to close the test window and click "Forward" to confirm the audio devices settings. The next screen will ask you to confirm the "Video Manager", it will default to the most appropriate selection so just click "Forward". Finally, the system will detect if you have a web camera attached and will confirm the device setting. Click "Forward" to confirm and you will be shown a summary of all the settings that Ekiga will use, as shown in Figure 8-5.

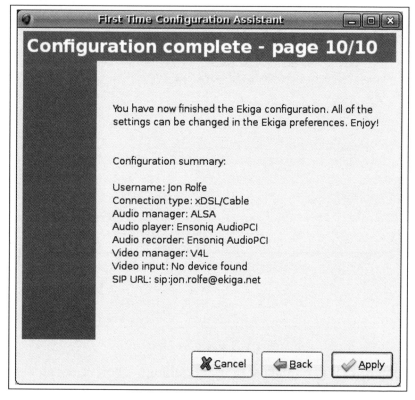

Figure 8-5 Configuration Complete

Make sure all the settings are correct and press the "Apply" button to configure and launch the application.

Using Ekiga

Once the application is configured, it can be used to make different types of calls to other users as long as you know their SIP address.

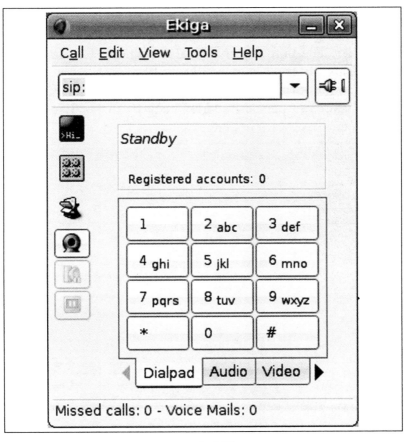

Figure 8-6 Ekiga

Along the top of the Ekiga window is a text box where you can manually enter a persons address, as can be seen in Figure 8-6. Then by clicking on the connect button next to the text box, Ekiga will attempt to call the other person. The buttons down the left-hand side of the window change how Ekiga will communicate, either using instant messaging, voice, or video conferencing if you have a web camera attached to your computer. The third button will also open the Ekiga address book. This will connect to the Ekiga SIP service and allow you to search for other Ekiga users SIP addresses, or allows you to create your own personal address book by manually entering their details, as shown in Figure 8-7.

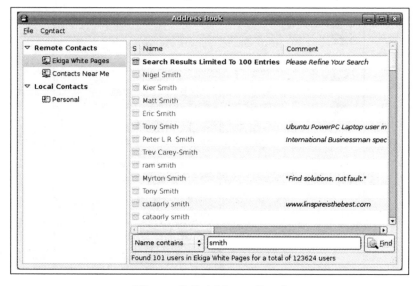

Figure 8-7 Address Book

Once Ekiga is launched, clicking the close button in its window will not actually close the application, but leave it minimised in the notification area of the top panel. This is necessary as you will only be able to receive calls while the application is running. Once the application is minimised to the notification area, simply left-click the small telephone icon to maximise the window. To really close the application, so that you are not disturbed, choose "Quit" from the "Call" menu.

Evolution Mail

Evolution (http://www.gnome.org/projects/evolution) is a fully featured email client which is pre-installed on Ubuntu, as shown in Figure 8-8. It can be launched from either the icon on the top panel or from the "Internet" sub-menu to the "Applications" menu. Evolution includes numerous features such as POP, SMTP, Exchange, GroupWise and multiple email account support, calendars including support for connecting to web based calendars, junk mail filtering, advanced inbuilt search facility, and support for plug-ins to add additional functionality.

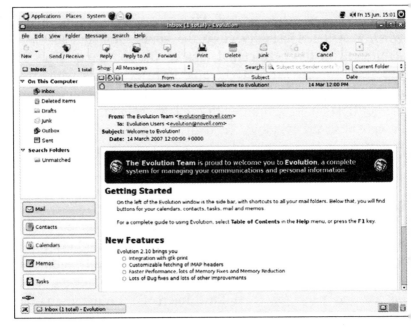

Figure 8-8 Evolution Mail

Like Ekiga, in order to make the set-up as easy as possible, Evolution launches a wizard the first time its started to step you through the configuration process to connect to your email host. Press the "Forward" button on the first page of the set-up assistant to start the configuration, as shown in Figure 8-9.

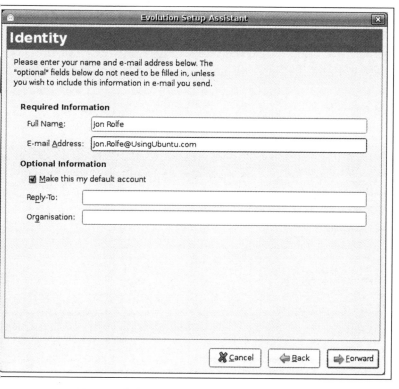

Figure 8-9 Evolution Set-up Assistant

Enter your full name as you wish it to be displayed on your emails, and your email address into the fields as shown in the previous illustration. The Reply-To and Organisation fields can normally be left blank and only need to be completed if you wish to use a different email address for users replying to your email, and you wish a company name to be entered into the properties of each email. Then click the "Forward" button to go to the email configuration account properties.

The fields on this page will vary depending on the email account that you are using. Evolution can support receiving email from many different server types, however for this book we will assume that you are connecting to an Internet Service Provider who, by and large, will provide a POP email service. When "POP" is selected, the options shown in Figure 8-10 will be displayed.

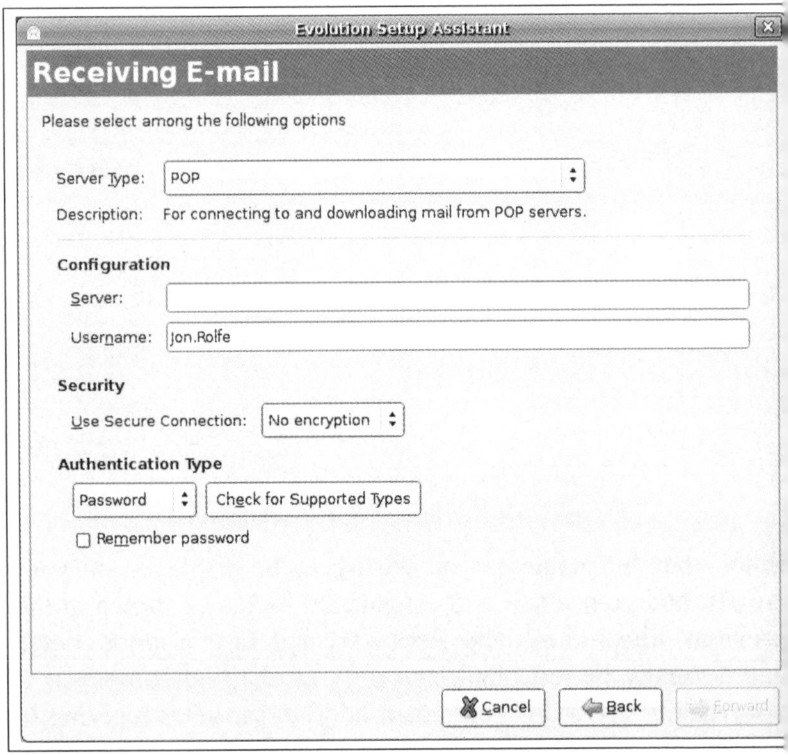

Figure 8-10 Receiving email

Enter the address of your email server and your user name, these will be provided to you by your Internet Service provider. Tick the "Remember Password" check box if you wish Evolution to remember your password so that it can automatically collect your email without prompting you to enter your password on each connection. Don't worry that you have not entered your password yet, Evolution will prompt you the first time it tries to receive email. Then click the "Forward" button to move onto the email receive options page.

Select how often you wish Evolution to check for email when it is running, and tick the check box to "Leave messages on server" if you want access to your email from several different computers, before clicking "Forward".

The next page allows you to set up your email settings in order to send email via your Internet Service Provider. Enter the server address, user name and tick the check box to "Remember Password". Some email servers will require the "Server requires authentication" option checked while others will not. Again, you may need to check with your ISP to find out if this is an option that needs to be ticked for your provider. Click "Forward" again to save the settings and go to the next page.

You will then be prompted to name the account settings to make it easier to manage if you have multiple email addresses. Change the name if necessary and click "Forward" to take you to the time zone setting page, as shown in Figure 8-11.

Figure 8-11 Time zone

This page should look familiar from the Ubuntu installation.

Click near your geographical region and then select you location, before clicking "Forward". On the final set-up page click "Apply" to save the account settings.

Using Evolution

If you have used an email client before, Evolution will be very easy to get started with. A tool bar shown along the top of the window allows you to create, send, receive, reply, forward or delete emails. Buttons down the left-hand side of the window allow you to switch between views so that you can look at your email, contacts, calendar, memos or tasks.

As you change the view, from email to calendar for instance, the tool bar buttons will change to actions of the view you are currently in. A small icon in the bottom left-hand corner of the window shows you if you are currently connected to your email server or not. Clicking the icon will allow you to change the connection status.

Firefox Web Browser

Ubuntu comes with the popular Firefox (http://www.mozilla.com/en-US/firefox) web browser which can be launched from either the icon on the top panel or from the "Internet" sub-menu of the "Applications" menu.

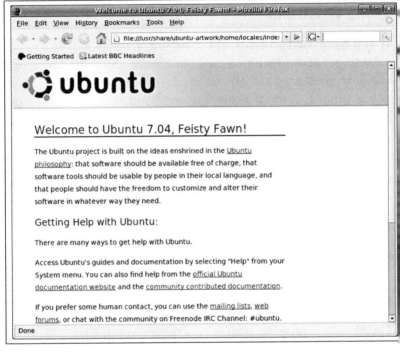

Figure 8-12 Firefox

Firefox uses a "tabbed" interface that allows you to either open a single web page per window, or to open a new page into a "tab" which will be shown along the top of the browser window under the address bar, and can be seen in Figure 8-12. This allows you to open multiple web pages without littering your desktop with multiple windows.

It also has the concept of "Live Bookmarks", these are displayed under the address bar but above the tabs. This feature allows you to "bookmark" automatically updating RSS feeds. These are feeds that push updates to your browser. When you create a Live Bookmark for a feed, you receive a drop-down menu that lists all the articles at the site in real time. As the articles change on the feed, the drop-down menu will automatically be updated.

There are very few settings that need to be changed to use Firefox, if you are connected to the Internet, Firefox can be used straight away to access the Web, and it functions like any other browser that you may have used. To search for a particular subject, enter a description into the search box in the top right corner of the window and the search results will be returned by the Google search engine. Alternatively, simply enter the web address into the address bar to go straight to a web site.

You may wish to customise some of the settings, and these can be changed by selecting "Preferences" from the "Edit" menu. On the Main preferences screen as shown in Figure 8-13, you can change your home page by entering a web site address into the home page field. Also on the same screen, you can change the default location to save files when they are downloaded.

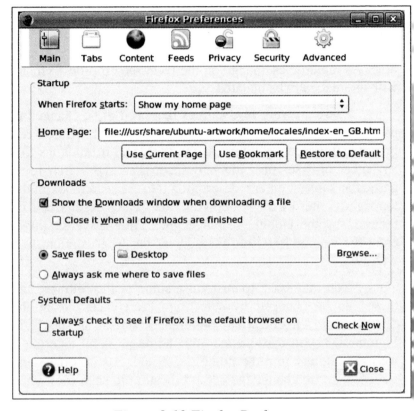

Figure 8-13 Firefox Preferences

On the Privacy page, as shown in Figure 8-14, you may also want to change how long Firefox remembers the websites you have visited. You can also clear your web usage information on this page by clicking the "Clear Now" button. Alternatively if you click the check box to clear your private data when you close Firefox, it will be removed automatically after each session.

Figure 8-14 Firefox Privacy Settings

Finally, on the Network tab of the Advanced page you can select how much data is cached or stored after visiting each site. This feature makes websites load faster if the data or pictures haven't changed since the last visit, and is very useful if you have a slow connection to the Internet. However, for security reasons or to save disc space, you may want to reduce the size of the cache used.

Also on this tab are the "Connections" settings, as shown in Figure 8-15. These settings allow you to connect through a proxy server. This is a server that routes your web page requests for you, this can be helpful for both security and performance reasons. Check with you ISP to find out if you need to configure proxy server setting.

Figure 8-15 Firefox Advanced Settings

Firefox makes it very easy to install plug-ins which you may need to view certain web pages. For instance, many pages use the Adobe Flash plug-in for web page animations. As this plug-in is copyrighted, it is not pre-installed in Ubuntu. However, whenever you navigate to a web page that requires a particular plug-in, Firefox will prompt that a plug-in is required by displaying a bar and button stating "Install Missing Plug ins". When you click the button, Firefox will search for the plug-in and step you through the process of installing it.

Gaim Internet Messenger

Gaim is an Instant Messaging application that can be used to send and receive real-time text messages to users of AIM, MSN, Yahoo, IRC and many other Instant Messaging applications. It has recently been renamed to Pidgin (http://pidgin.im), but at the time of writing, the new version is not yet available for Ubuntu.

Like many of the applications installed on Ubuntu, when you run Gaim for the first time it starts an assistant in order to configure it with an existing Instant Messenger (IM) account. You need to create an account with an Instant Message service before you can configure Gaim. The advantage of this application is it can support multiple accounts on different services, so if you have friends and family using different applications, you can create an account on each service and configure Gaim to use all the services simultaneously.

Currently, Gaim supports the following IM platforms:

- AIM
- Gadu-Gadu
- GroupWise
- ICQ
- IRC
- Jabber
- MSN
- Simple (SIP)
- Yahoo.

Once you have an IM account, start Gaim from the "Internet" sub-menu of the "Applications" menu. You will then be shown the Gaim welcome screen, as shown in Figure 8-16.

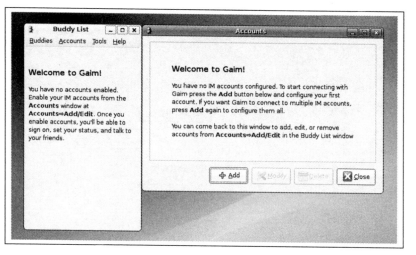

Figure 8-16 Gaim Account Set-up

Click the "Add" button and then choose the type of account you want to set up from the drop-down list, as shown in Figure 8-17.

> The exact details you will need to enter will vary according to the type of the account, as many settings will be pre-configured for the popular types of service.

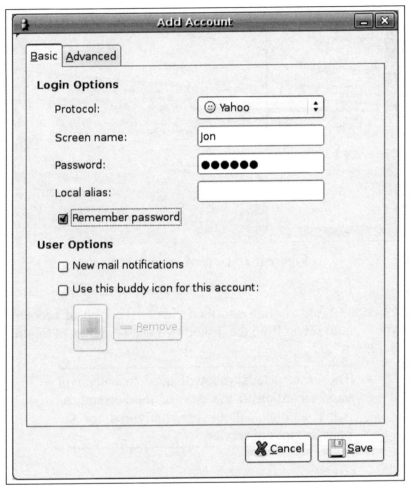

Figure 8-17 Gaim Add Account

Once you have configured the account, click the "Save" button. The application will then try to connect to the service, if it is unsuccessful, select the account in the "Accounts" window and click modify to review the settings you have entered.

Once the account successfully connects you will need to add friends to the application so that you can contact them and see their status as on-line (available), off-line or busy. You can add friends by choosing "Add Buddy" from the "Buddies" menu, as shown in Figure 8-18.

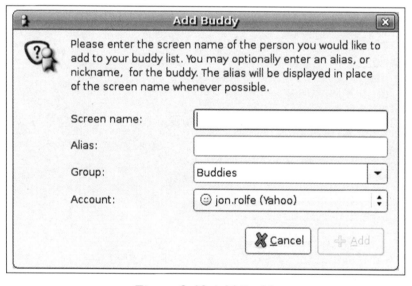

Figure 8-18 Add Buddy

To contact another person you will need to know their account name for the relative service.

If you are not sure of the account name and the service your buddies are using just ask them.

Select the account from the drop-down list of your configured accounts and enter the user's account name or screen name. Then give the user an "Alias" which Gaim will use to display in the application window or "Buddy List". Whenever you try to add an account to your buddy list, or if someone adds you to their buddy list, the user being added will be asked to authorise or approve being entered into the other person's buddy list. This is to ensure that only users that you approve of can monitor your on-line status.

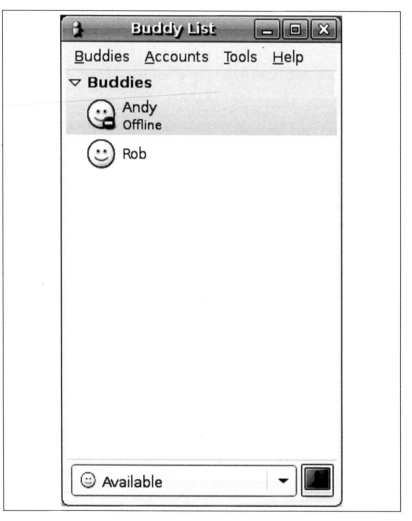

Figure 8-19 Buddy List

Once you have a few friends in your buddy list, their status will be displayed, as shown in Figure 8-19. This allows you to see who is available to talk to. You can change your status, so you are not interrupted when you are busy, from the pop-up menu at the bottom of the buddy list window. To talk to a user who is available, simply double-click their name and type into the conversation window, as shown in Figure 8-20.

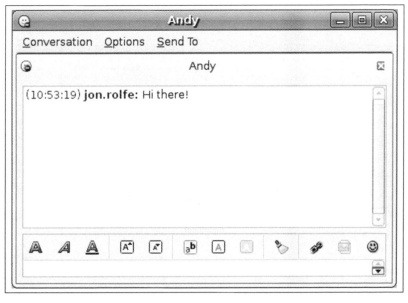

Figure 8-20 Conversation window

You can only be contacted by someone while the Gaim application is running, so the Gaim windows can be closed without actually closing the application. While Gaim is in this state, it will add an icon in the notification area of the top panel. To really close the application, right-click the icon and choose quit from the drop-down menu.

Summary

You should now be able to send and receive emails, browse the Internet, and as long as you know other people with Instant Messaging or VOIP accounts, you can send text, voice or video messages in real time.

Even though Ubuntu is a free operating system, we have found that it includes all the functionality of other expensive operating systems. In fact, due to the open source nature of the GNU/Linux platform, the applications available offer a greater level of flexibility than some commercial applications by supporting multiple accounts to different services, such as being able to communicate with users on different Instant Messaging services using a single application like Gaim.

9

Sound and Video

Ubuntu is a fully-featured multi-media operating system, and as such it comes complete with tools to watch videos, play music and convert CDs to digital audio files. In this chapter we try out the applications in the "Sound & Video" sub-menu of the "Applications" menu.

Totem

Totem (http://www.gnome.org/projects/totem) is the standard open source movie player for the GNOME desktop environment and is launched from the "Movie Player" short cut in the "Sounds & Video" sub-menu. It features a play list, video thumbnailer for file management, a full-screen mode, seek and volume controls, keyboard navigation and DVD (without encryption) playback.

Figure 9-1 Totem

Using Totem is easy and it can play a variety of file types by simply double-clicking the file. You can try this now by navigating to the "Examples" folder in your home directory and double-clicking the "Experience ubuntu.ogg" file, as shown in Figure 9-1. Alternatively, you can open a video or music file from within Totem using the standard "Open" command on the "Movie" menu. Its also possible to use Totem to play "streaming" video, this is video that is streamed from a web server. You can play streaming video by selecting "Open location..." from the "Movie" menu and entering the full address to the video stream.

The Totem window is split into several areas. The display area is used to show the video or a visualisation while an audio file is playing. The sidebar on the left-hand side is used to display the properties of the playing file or to display a play list. Along the bottom of the Totem window are the player seek controls, volume and time bar.

Totem, and other video player applications, use software called "codecs" to play different digital video files and streaming media types.

A codec (meaning compression-decompression or coder-decoder) is a small piece of software for encoding and decoding a digital file or stream.

Totem comes with many codecs pre-installed, but from time to time you may encounter a file type that Totem does not support as it requires a copyrighted codec that is not installed.

If you try to open a file or DVD or CD disc which Totem does not have the codec for, it may automatically start the "Add/Remove Applications" utility and prompt you to install a particular codec if it recognises which one is missing, as shown in Figure 9-2. Alternatively, it may just prompt you to install the codec. In which case, open the "Add/Remove Applications" utility and simply type "codec" into the search field. This will list the available codecs and list the file types that they support, Totem can support any of the "Gstreamer" or "Xine" type codecs.

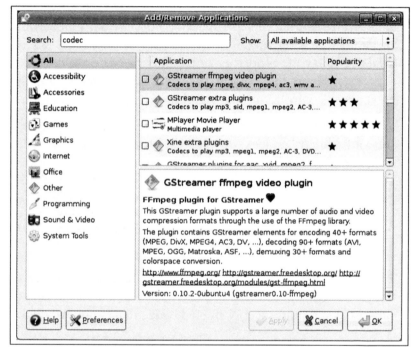

Figure 9-2 Add/Remove Applications

Its also recommended that you change the network connection option under the Totem preferences, as shown in Figure 9-3. This allows Totem to optimise its settings for your type of

Internet connection, and can be achieved by selecting "Preferences" from the "Edit" menu. On the "General" tab of the "Preferences" window select the connection type that corresponds with your Internet connection.

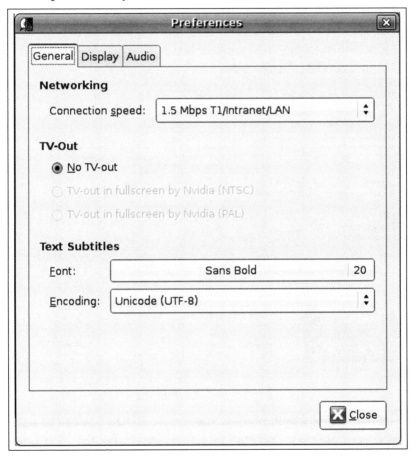

Figure 9-3 Preferences

Rhythmbox Music Player

The Rhythmbox box application (http://www.gnome.org/projects/rhythmbox) is used to play audio CDs and manage and play music files, podcasts and Internet based radio stations, as shown in Figure 9-4. It is launched from the "Rhythmbox Music Player" short cut in the "Sound & Video" sub-menu.

Figure 9-4 Rhythmbox

The first time Rhythmbox is started, an assistant is run to help you configure the application, its recommended that you have a "Music" and "Podcasts" directory in your home directory before running the assistant. On the first screen, click "Forward". You will then be prompted for the directory containing any existing music files you have and to use if you create new audio files from a CD, as shown in Figure 9-5. Either browse to the location or type the path into the box, and click "Forward".

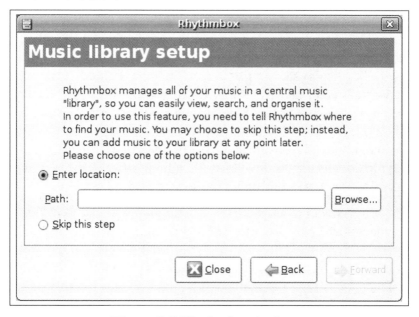

Figure 9-5 Rhythmbox Assistant

On the final assistant screen, click "Apply" to save the settings and the application will open. The Rhythmbox window is split into several different areas. Along the top of the window are the menu and tool bar which provides access to the player functions such as play, pause and stop. The window itself is split into a source list pane on the left-hand side that shows the different types of sources such as music, Internet radio, podcasts and play lists, and also a graphic showing album artwork. The rest of the window is a browser allowing you to browse the different types of media. Finally, along the bottom of the window is a status bar showing information relating to the current selected or playing source.

If you have an existing music collection in digital file format, you will need to import it into Rhythmbox before it will be displayed, simply select "Import Folder" from the "Music" menu and Rhythmbox will use the files and display them in the source list. Playing music is easy by selecting an individual file, album or artist and clicking play. When Rhythmbox plays an album for the first time, it will automatically try to download the album artwork for you and display it in a window under the source list.

As well as music files, Rhythmbox will also download podcasts and play Internet radio. Adding a new Radio station can be completed by clicking the "Radio" source and then choosing "New Internet Radio Station" from the "Music" menu. Then type the address or "URL" of the Internet radio station into the text box and click OK. The new Radio will then be listed in the source list and can be played by selecting it and clicking the "play" button. Similarly, podcasts can be added in the same way by choosing the "New Podcast Feed" from the "Music" menu and then entering the URL into the text box. Each new episode of the podcast will be automatically downloaded when its detected by Rhythmbox and stored in your "Podcast" directory. Once the file is downloaded it can be played just like a music file.

Serpentine

The Serpentine application (http://s1x.homelinux.net/projects/serpentine/) is an easy to use utility for creating audio CDs from music files. It supports multiple digital file formats (WAV, MP3, OGG, FLAC) as well as dragging and dropping files from the file manager or the Rhythmbox application. The application is launched from the "Serpentine" icon in the "Sound & Video" sub-menu.

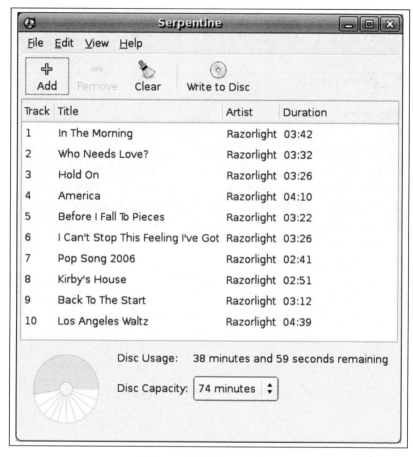

Figure 9-6 Serpentine

When started, the easy to use interface as shown in Figure 9-6 is displayed. Simply drag and drop files from the Rhythmbox application or from the File Manager into the Serpentine window. Alternatively, either click the "Add" button on the tool bar and browse for music files or a play list file. Once the files are selected, simply click the "Write to disc" button to start to create an audio CD. Like the Totem application, Serpentine uses "codecs" to decode the music files and write them to the CD. If the correct codec is not installed, an error message will be produced warning you that the file types are not supported.

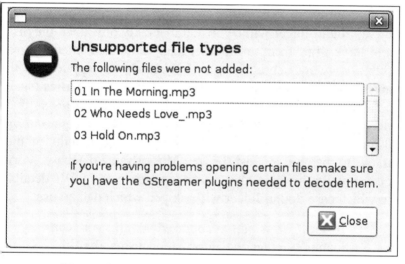

Figure 9-7 Serpentine Unsupported file types

Simply use the "Add/Remove Applications" utility to search for the file extension (such as "MP3") and the correct codec will be displayed, tick the check box to select the codec and click "OK" to install it. Once the codec is installed, if you restart the Serpentine application it will now be able to read the file format and create the CD.

Sound Juicer

This application is used for extracting or "ripping" music from an audio CD and converting it to a digital audio file that can be played with the Rhythmbox or Totem applications. It can also be used to play CD audio discs directly on your computer. Sound Juicer can be seen in Figure 9-8.

When a CD is loaded into your computers CD or DVD drive, Sound Juicer will try to automatically download the disc and track titles from an Internet database called MusicBrainz (http://www.musicbrainz.org). This allows the application to automatically name the audio files and assign properties (such as album title, track title, artist, etc) to the audio files so that they will be displayed when played. The CD is recognised by using its serial number and the positions and lengths of the tracks to match it against the free MusicBrainz database. Very occasionally this data may return more than one CD's details, in which case Sound Juicer will ask you which data to use.

If the CD is not recognised at all, you can manually enter the information using the title, artist and genre text fields.

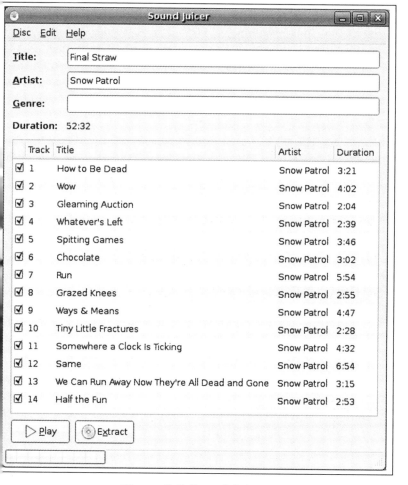

Figure 9-8 Sound Juicer

Before converting a CD to an audio file for the first time, select the "Preferences" option from the "Edit" menu to select the directory you wish to store the new files in, and the type of file format that you want to create. Serpentine supports many types of format such as FLAC, OGG, MP, ACC and WAV. Before choosing a format, ensure that the format you use is compatible with any portable music players that you wish to use. Generally the MP3 format is widely used, however it has a lower sound quality but smaller file size than the FLAC format for example. Once you have chosen the directory and the file type to use, click the "Extract" button. The new files will be created in a directory structure in the format "Artist Name" then a sub-directory of "Album Title".

Sound Recorder

The Sound Recorder application is a utility that allows you to record audio files if you have a microphone attached to your computer, as shown in Figure 9-9. Select the audio format from the drop-down list and then just click the "Record" button to start the recording and click the "Stop" button to complete the recording. The new audio file can then be saved by clicking the "Save" button.

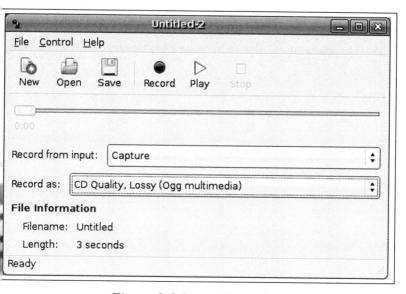

Figure 9-9 Sound Recorder

Summary

Sound and Video files are becoming more and more popular as connections to the Internet are becoming faster, and they allow anyone to start broadcasting using "podcasts". As we have seen, Ubuntu has the tools to play either local media files such as home videos or music, or to stream the media such as Internet Radio stations or video clips, and can even download the files automatically for you such as podcasts. You have also now discovered the major applications that are included as standard with Ubuntu, however there are many more available through the "Add/Remove Applications" utility for you to discover. Some of these applications will provide different tools to perform the same function as we have already discovered, however there are also lots more to perform small niche tasks that you may find useful. Simply use the search function as described earlier for installing "Codecs" to look for applications that you might find of use.

PART 4
Troubleshooting

10

Finding Help

In this final chapter, we look into how to find help to solve problems that might occur while you are using Ubuntu. We will review the on-line help in Ubuntu and the installed applications, and also cover the resources on the Internet, including further documentation and help forums.

Ubuntu Help Centre

The "Ubuntu Help Centre" is the on-line help manual that can be launched from the question mark icon on the top panel.

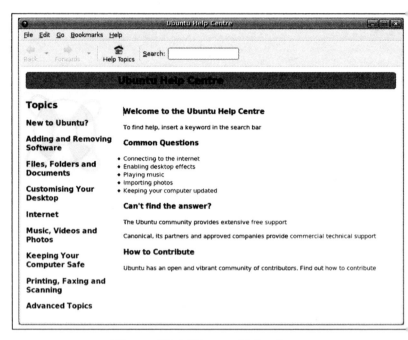

Figure 10-1 Ubuntu Help Centre

The Help Centre is a hypertext style help manual which lists topics down the left-hand side and links to common questions in the main window, as shown in Figure 10-1. It also includes a link to the free Ubuntu support forum which allows specific questions to be asked of the Ubuntu community.

> Searching through and posting questions to the Ubuntu community through the Ubuntu support forum is a great way to get help.

A search field on the tool bar is provided for searching for specific topics if they are not listed on the main help page, and a "Help Topics", "Forward" and "Back" buttons allow you to navigate through the documentation and will return you to the main page.

When you click one of the topics on the main page, an index pane is opened on the left-hand side to display the individual sub-topics and the first page of the topic is displayed in the main window. The Ubuntu Help Centre should be your first port of call for Ubuntu help as it includes:

- An introduction to Ubuntu 7.04

- Adding and removing software

- Using the File Manager

- Customising the desktop

- Using music, videos and photos

- How to keep your computer safe

- Printing, faxing and scanning

- Advanced topics.

Application Help

Within each of the installed applications, help specific to the application you are using can be launched by selecting the help option from the "Help" menu. This option can either start the Ubuntu Help Centre with the appropriate topic loaded, or it may start a help application specific to the application, such as the Firefox web browser help shown in Figure 10-2.

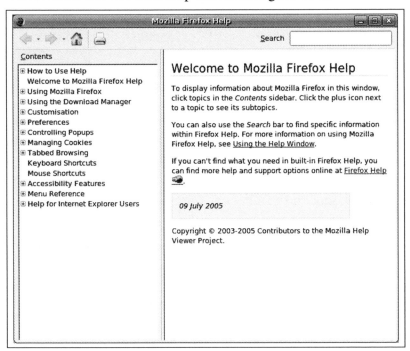

Figure 10-2 Firefox Help

In either case, navigating the application help or the Ubuntu Help Centre is very similar, with topics shown in the right-hand pane and the index in the left-hand. The tool bar will also include the same search, forward, back and home buttons.

Some applications will also include links on the "Help" menu to their Internet sites for more extensive documentation or help forums. For instance the OpenOffice.org Writer application includes a "Support" option on the "Help" menu which will launch Firefox and display the Ubuntu help site for OpenOffice.org.

Internet Based Documentation

If the on-line help does not answer your query, the Ubuntu community includes extensive Internet based documentation, forums or tutorials.

Ubuntu Documentation

The official Ubuntu site includes an Internet based version of the Ubuntu Help Centre (https://help.ubuntu.com), which includes the same help and documentation as included within the Ubuntu system

Ubuntu Community Documentation

Ubuntu community users and developers have extended the official documentation on the Ubuntu User Documentation site (https://help.ubuntu.com/community). This site should be your second help resource if you cannot find the answer to your question in the official documentation. An example of this site can be seen in Figure 10-3.

Figure 10-3 Ubuntu User Community Documentation

As well as providing help for installing, configuring and using Ubuntu, this site also lists other applications that can be installed, as well as the installation instructions.

GNOME Documentation

As we have already discovered, many of the applications and the GNOME desktop environment are common between different versions of the GNU/Linux operating systems. You can therefore find additional help resources at the web sites for each of the Open Source applications. For instance, the GNOME desktop environment includes extensive documentation at the GNOME website (http://www.gnome.org/support). This includes documentation and forums for the GNOME workspace, file manager, applications and system administration and an example can be seen in Figure 10-4.

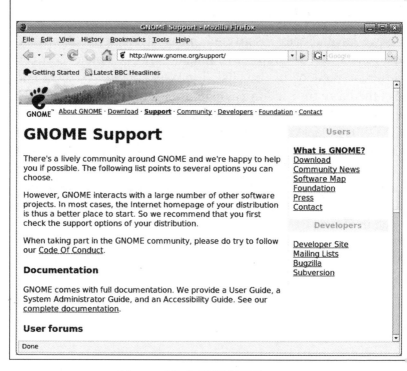

Figure 10-4 GNOME Support

Application Documentation

Finally, specific applications within Ubuntu will also provide additional documentation on their own websites, such as the OpenOffice.org suite, Firefox or GIMP. A complete list of web sites for the installed applications are listed in the chapters discussion each of the applications.

Help Forums

If after reading all the on-line help and documentation you still have problems, the Ubuntu community can help with Internet base forums specialising in Ubuntu, GNOME and Linux.

Ubuntu Forums

The official Ubuntu forums are available in many languages from the main Ubuntu site (http://www.ubuntu.com/support/community/webforums). However, the English language forum can be found at http://ubuntuforums.org. The forums are now run and maintained by Canonical Ltd, and allow users to post messages and receive free help from fellow users, developers and experts.

Commercial Help

There are many organisations that provide commercial support for open source software, and Canonical Ltd provides paid-for support for Ubuntu desktop, server and thin client systems. This support can be either working hours or complete 24 hour support which includes email and phone support, and is ideal for large deployments and installation advice. More information is available from the Ubuntu website (http://www.ubuntu.com/support/paid).

Summary

In this chapter you have seen that Ubuntu has numerous sources of help. From the on-line help within the operating system, to the application specific help, Internet based community documentation and finally the Ubuntu forums where you can post problems for Ubuntu users and experts to resolve.

PART 5
Appendix and Glossary

Appendix

The following table lists the Web site addresses that have been mentioned throughout the book which provide additional help, support or tutorial resources that might be of interest to the Ubuntu user.

Web site	URL
Debian	http://www.debian.org
Edubuntu Official Site	http://www.edubuntu.org
Ekiga Softphone	http://www.gnomemeeting.org
Evolution Email	http://www.gnome.org/projects/evolution
Firefox Web Browser	http://www.mozilla.com/en-US/firefox

Web site	URL
Free Software Foundation	http://www.fsf.org
F-Spot Photo Manager	http://f-spot.org
Gimp Documentation	http://www.gimp.org/docs
Gimp Photo Editor	http://www.gimp.org
Gimp Tutorials	http://www.gimp.org/tutorials
GNOME	http://www.gnome.org
GNOME Character Map	http://live.gnome.org/Gucharmap
GNOME Support	http://www.gnome.org/support
GNOME Text Editor	http://www.gedit.org
GNU Project	http://www.gnu.org
gThumb Image Viewer	http://gthumb.sourceforge.net

Web site	URL
Kubuntu Official Site	http://www.kubuntu.org
OpenOffice.org	http://openoffice.org
OpenOffice.org Documentation	http://documentation.openoffice.org
Pidgin (Formally Gaim)	http://pidgin.im
Rhythmbox Music Player	http://www.gnome.org/projects/rhythmbox
Serpentine Audio CD Creator	http://developer.berlios.de/projects/serpentine
Tomboy Notes	http://www.gnome.org/projects/tomboy
Totem Movie Player	http://www.gnome.org/projects/totem
Ubuntu Commercial Support	http://www.ubuntu.com/support/paid

Web site	URL
Ubuntu Community Documentation	https://help.ubuntu.com/community
Ubuntu Download Page	http://www.ubuntu.com/getubuntu/downl oad
Ubuntu Official Site	http://www.ubuntu.com
Ubuntu Stockists	http://www.ubuntu.com/getubuntu/purcha se
Ubuntu Studio Official Site	http://ubuntustudio.com
Ubuntu Support Forums	http://ubuntuforums.org
Using Ubuntu Blog	http://usingubuntu.com
Xubuntu Official Site	http://www.xubuntu.org

Glossary

Term	Definition
Advanced Audio Coding (AAC)	Digital audio format used for streaming audio and music files
America Online Instant Messenger (AIM)	Instant messenger application provided and run by the America On-Line (AOL) Internet Service Provider
American Standard Code for Information Interchange (ASCII)	Character coding standard based on the English language
Asynchronous Digital Subscriber Line (ADSL)	Technology used for transmitting digital information at high speeds on existing copper phone lines

Term	Definition
Basic Input/Output System (BIOS)	Software built in to the computer motherboard which controls the system hardware, allowing the computer to start up and launch the operating system from the hard disc
C	Programming language
C++	Object oriented version of the C programming language
Compact Disc (CD)	Optical digital storage format designed by Philips and Sony, commonly used for storing digital audio
Compact Disc Read-Only Memory (CD-Rom)	Optical digital storage data format based on compact disc media
Compact Disc-Recordable (CD-R)	Recordable optical digital storage format based on the compact disc format
Compressor-Decompressor (Codec)	Software or hardware used to convert from analogue to digital or digital to analogue formats

Term	Definition
dBase	Database application
Distribution	The name used for a particular GNU/Linux version
Domain Name System (DNS)	A system for converting host names into IP addresses
Dynamic Host Configuration Protocol (DHCP)	Protocol for automatically assigning IP addresses to systems
Dynamic Versatile Disc (DVD)	Optical digital storage format used for storing data and video
Extensible Markup Language (XML)	World Wide Web Consortium specification for the exchange of data
Free Lossless Audio Codec (FLAC)	Digital audio format used for streaming audio and music files, allows compression of the audio without losing data
GNU	Meaning "GNU's Not Unix", a project started to develop a free open-source operating system and applications

Term	Definition
GNU Object Model Environment (GNOME)	Desktop environment used on GNU/Linux systems
GStreamer	Multimedia framework used by applications on the GNOME desktop environment
Hypersonic SQL Project Database (HSQLDB)	Relational database format
HyperText Markup Language (HTML)	File format used by the World Wide Web
I Seek You (ICQ)	Type of chat or instant messenger program
Instant Message (IM)	Message received through chat or "Instant Messaging" application
Integrated Services Digital Network (ISDN)	Technology used for transmitting digital information on existing copper phone lines

Term	Definition
International Standards Organization (ISO)	International organisation that maintains technology standards; the "ISO" file format is used to store images of compact discs
Internet Protocol (IP)	Protocol used to allow the communication and transfer of data across networks
Internet Relay Chat (IRC)	Type of chat or instant messenger software
Internet Service Provider (ISP)	Company providing access to the Internet
Java	Platform independent object oriented computer programming language
K Desktop Environment (KDE)	Desktop environment used on GNU/Linux systems
Kernel	The core of an operating system
Linux	Commonly used for the free open-source operating system, more correctly used to refer to the "kernel" used by the GNU/Linux operating system

Term	Definition
Local Area Network (LAN)	A local computer network, such as in a home or office
Microsoft Network (MSN)	Internet Service Provider and web portal run by Microsoft
Moving Picture Experts Group (MPEG)	A working group of the International Standard Organisation which concentrates on video and audio formats; also used to refer to a standard for the compression and storage of motion video
MPEG Layer 3 (MP3)	Digital audio format used for audio and music files
MySQL	Open-source database application
Nautilus	GNOME file manager application
Network Time Protocol (NTP)	Protocol used to synchronise time between different computers
Ogg	Open standard file format for audio and video media
Oracle	Commercial database application

Term	Definition
Portable Document Format (PDF)	File format used by the Adobe Acrobat application
Portable Network Graphics (PNG)	Open standard file format for compressed graphics
Post Office Protocol (POP)	Protocol used to receive mail from a server by a client
Practical Extraction and Report Language (Perl)	Programming language specifically designed for processing text
Rich Text Format (RTF)	Standard file format used for exporting text and formatting between applications
Session Initiation Protocol (SIP)	Protocol used for voice and multimedia used in telecoms or messaging applications
Simple Mail Transfer Protocol (SMTP)	Protocol used between message servers and to send messages from a client application

Term	Definition
Synaptic	GNOME application for installing/removing applications
Third Extended File System (EXT3)	File system format used by GNU/Linux systems
Transport Control Protocol (TCP)	Protocol used in combination with the Internet Protocol to allow communication between computers
Universal Resource Locator (URL)	Address of a web based resource on the Internet
Universal Serial Bus (USB)	Hardware standard used for the connection of peripherals to a computer
UNIX	Computer operating system developed by AT&T
Voice Over IP (VOIP)	Protocol used to send voice over the Internet Protocol
Waveform Audio (WAV)	Microsoft developed format for audio files
Wide Area Network (WAN)	Computer network that spans a large distance

Term	**Definition**
WiFi Protected Access (WPA)	Security protocol for wireless networks, designed to fix the security limitations of the WEP standard
Wired Equivalency Privacy (WEP)	Security protocol for wireless networks, now considered less secure than the newer WPA protocol
Xine	Multimedia format developed for UNIX but released under the GNU licence

Index

Notes

Notes

15 04 09

Take a note of the configuration details for your equipment for future reference:

Ubuntu version:

IP address:

Subnet mask:

Default gateway:

DNS Domain:

DNS addresses (if applicable):

Wireless Network ID (SSID):

 Network Key (WEP/WPA):

Printer details:

Any other information:

•